Revelations

The Autobiography
of Alvin Ailey

by ALVIN AILEY
with A.PETER BAILEY

REPLICA BOOKS

A DVISION OF BAKER & TAYLOR
BRIDGEWATER, NJ

FIRST REPLICA BOOKS EDITION, FEBRUARY 1999

Published by Replica Books, a division of Baker & Taylor,
1200 Route 22 East, Bridgewater, NJ 08807

Replica Books is a trademark of Baker & Taylor

Biographical Note

This Replica books edition, first published in 1999, is an
unabridged republication of the work first published
by Citadel Press, Carol Publishing Group, New Jersey in 1997

Baker & Taylor Cataloging-in-Publication Data

Ailey, Alvin.
Revelations : the autobiography of Alvin Ailey /
by Alvin Ailey with A. Peter Bailey. —1st Replica
Books ed.
p.   cm.
ISBN 0735100802
Originally published: Secaucus, N.J. : Carol Pub. Group,
c1995.
Includes index.
1. Ailey, Alvin. 2. Dancers - United States - Biography.
3. Choreographers - United States - Biography. I. Bailey,
A. Peter. II. Title.
GV1785.A38 A3 1999
792.8'092 [B]—dc 21

Manufactured in the United States of America

Revelations

$\mathcal{R}$evelations

The Autobiography of Alvin Ailey

by Alvin Ailey

WITH A. PETER BAILEY

A CITADEL PRESS BOOK
Published by Carol Publishing Group

Carol Publishing Group Edition, 1997

A Citadel Press Book
Published by Carol Publishing Group
Citadel Press is a registered trademark of Carol Communications, Inc.

Editorial, sales and distribution, rights and permissions inquiries should
be addressed to Carol Publishing Group, 120 Enterprise Avenue,
Secaucus, N.J. 07094

In Canada: Canadian Manda Group, One Atlantic Avenue, Suite 105,
Toronto, Ontario M6K 3E7

Carol Publishing Group books may be purchased in bulk at special
discounts for sales promotion, fund-raising, or educational purposes.
Special editions can be created to specifications. For details, contact:
Special Sales Department, Carol Publishing Group, 120 Enterprise
Avenue, Secaucus, N.J. 07094.

To Mrs. Lula Cooper, my mother

To Calvin Cooper, my brother

To Carmen de Lavallade and Brother John Sellers,
my great friends

Contents

CONTENTS

Foreword by Lena Horne

I first saw Alvin Ailey in the early 1950s in Los Angeles when I was asked to come in and make publicity pictures with some of the young people in his dance group. And there was Alvin, whom I was thrilled to meet for the first time because he was an absolutely beautiful and vital dancer. He was partnering Carmen de Lavallade, and it was such a joy to look at their talent and beauty. It was the first time I had seen dancers' power and passion combined with such lyricism.

A few years later I saw Alvin again. I was working in a Broadway musical called *Jamaica*, and the cast included some of the most beautiful, talented, committed dancers I had ever seen, and this was my first experience in working with groups of dancers. I saw in a multiracial cast such perseverance, such hunger, such talent, and such underexposure. I didn't know anything about the hardships the dancers had to go through, not only because they were dancers but also because it was so hard for the arts to be recognized, appreciated, and promoted. I selfishly had thought only about how tough it was getting along as an actress and a performer; I had forgotten that all the arts had a history of hard times and continue to have hard times. When I saw those young people, without money, without encouragement, going to class every day, studying, always moving, torturing their bodies, and continually learning, they inspired me to better prepare myself for the life I had to lead as a black artist in a society that too often refuses to recognize and reward fine talent and its contributions to our culture.

In *Jamaica,* Alvin looked to me like a young football player. He was so huge and beautifully built and full of energy. All of the dancers were as talented as he was, probably, and maybe a few even more so, but no one loved work more or worked harder to learn than he did. Because of his look, like a young lion and yet like an earth man, I began to call him "Earth Man." He always spoke of the fact that our strength came to us through the bottoms of our feet, through the earth, through the floor, and that was the way I always saw my art from then on, as though I were planted in the earth and trying to push the sound of my music up through my body, from the earth. So I will never forget him.

I began to talk to Alvin a lot, and he told me about a company he was trying to put together. He asked if I'd come to see a concert he was going to give at the Young Men's Hebrew Association on Ninety-second Street in Manhattan. I went that afternoon and was captivated by what I saw and experienced. I now saw that he was equally creative as a choreographer and a dancer. He put his whole soul into his dancing, and it was obvious that when it came to dance on any level, he never stopped. He never stopped creating. It was all or nothing.

That concern made me a devoted admirer and supporter of Alvin and his company, and I have remained so for over thirty years. I see the Alvin Ailey American Dance Theater perform as often as I can, and I never cease to be amazed by Alvin's thinking and passion for dance, especially black dance. Alvin's combination of great talent and energizing passion compelled me to respond to the first concert of his that I saw. His ballets still do that today, more than five years after his death. And that's why the Earth Man's legacy to dance is eternal.

Introduction by A. Peter Bailey

*D*uring an interview in early 1988, I asked Alvin Ailey to describe himself. After a brief hesitation, he said: "My feelings about myself have been terrible. The whole of where I came from, the Brazos Valley in Texas, picking cotton in my early life, being with my mother and not with my father, living through the 1930s, the lack of a real father, not having enough food sometimes, going around to those churches and the Dew Drop Inns, all left an enormous stain and a sense of inferiority that lasted for many years. I felt that no matter what I did, what ballet I made, how beautifully I danced, it was not good enough. Even now I doubt whether the new ballet is going to be what it really should be—even though I've made 150 ballets. That's one of the worst things about racism, what it does to young people. It tears down your insides so that no matter what you achieve, no matter what you write or choreograph, you feel it's not quite enough. You're not quite up to snuff.

"One of the aspects of my personality is that I always want more. I always want to have more dancers in my company. I want to do bigger ballets; I want to have live music. I want all those things, and sometimes when you don't get them, you feel bad about yourself when there's no reason to. I know that feelings of inferiority from way back have run throughout my whole career. No matter what I'm doing, dancing in *House of Flowers* or dancing with Carmen de Lavallade, these feelings stay with me. One of the processes of your life is to constantly break that down, to constantly reaffirm that I Am Somebody."

What Alvin left out of this honest self-analysis is that he was also a world-class choreographer whose masterpiece, *Revelations,* may well have been seen by more people than any other ballet created in the twentieth century. Jimmy Truitte, a former Ailey dancer and one of Alvin's longtime friends, still marvels at memories of a concert in Germany where the company took an incredible sixty curtain calls after dancing *Revelations*. "It was astounding," said Truitte. "To stop them we finally had to go upstage and walk downstage very, very, very slowly, bow again, and then back up at the same tempo. It was only then that the audience stopped applauding."

Alvin was also a man whose company, at the time of his death, had performed for an estimated 15 million people in forty-eight states and forty-five countries on six continents. It was also a company that, in its then thirty years of existence, had performed 150 ballets by fifty choreographers, thus living up to Alvin's goal of seeing that great ballets "were not lost—built upon, but not lost." Noted black dance historian Joe Nash wrote: "Alvin is unique in the whole history of dance because he had over fifty choreographers make works for his company. That means his dancers have to be trained so that they can move from jazz to ballet to ethnic to abstract to postmodern minimalist. You name it. That establishes the Ailey group as unique in the whole history of dance."

Alvin created ballets not only for the Alvin Ailey American Dance Theatre (AAADT) but also for other notable companies, including American Ballet Theatre, Royal Danish Ballet, London Festival Ballet, the Joffrey Ballet, Paris Opera Ballet, and La Scala Opera Ballet. He also choreographed Samuel Barber's *Anthony and Cleopatra,* which opened the Metropolitan Opera's inaugural season at the Lincoln Center for the Performing Arts in New York City in 1966, and Leonard Bernstein's *Mass,* which opened the Kennedy Center for the Performing Arts in Washington, D.C., in 1971.

His awards included first prize at the International Dance Festival in Paris (1970), the Dance Magazine Award (1975), the NAACP Spingarn Medal (1976), the New York City Mayor's Award for Arts and Culture (1977), the Capezio Award (1979), the Samuel H. Scripps American Dance Festival Award (1987), and the Kennedy Center Award (1988). The Spingarn Medal is given for "the highest and noblest achievement by an American Negro during the previous year or years," and the Scripps Award, modern dance's most prestigious prize, is given for lifetime contribution to the field.

His company garnered several significant firsts: It was the first black dance company sent abroad under President John F. Kennedy's International Exchange Program (1962); the first American modern dance company to perform in the Soviet Union since the days of Isadora Duncan (1970); the first black modern dance company to perform at the Metropolitan Opera (1983); and the first modern dance company to make a U.S. government–sponsored tour of the People's Republic of China after the normalization of Sino–American relations (1985).

I first saw the AAADT perform in 1968. I was then beginning a stint as an assistant editor at *Ebony* magazine. Lerone Bennett Jr., the senior editor at the time, was writing an article on the emerging black student movement on predominantly white college campuses. Black students at Dartmouth College had scheduled their first Black Weekend in February 1968, and I was sent to Hanover, New Hampshire, to cover the event. Among the groups invited to participate was the AAADT. This was to be my first viewing of what is called concert dance. I had very little idea of what to expect, having had only a short time to read up on Alvin's company.

A true artist's vision forever changes the way one looks at his art, even if it covers territory that one is familiar with. Alvin and his company accomplished that for us with their performance at Dartmouth. After watching his company perform, I could never again look at dance in the same way, and after seeing *Revelations* I could never hear spirituals the same way. Through their beautiful, moving, and inspiring performing, Alvin and his company extensively and dramatically broadened my concept of dance.

During interviews I found others who were also dazzled upon seeing the AAADT perform for the first time. Award-winning choreographer and former Ailey dancer George Faison was a student at Howard University in Washington, D.C., when he saw the Ailey troupe for the first time. He remembers: "The curtain opened, and my life flowed out from the wings. I had never seen anything like it in my life—the energy, the bearing." Judith Jamison, a superb Ailey dancer who succeeded Alvin as the company's artistic director, was a student at the Philadelphia Dance Academy when she saw the AAADT for the first time. She still remembers the awe it produced in her and fellow students in her improvisation classes at the Academy. "For the first three weeks after seeing the Alvin Ailey American Dance Theatre, no one did anything original. All we did was what we thought we had seen onstage."

It's fascinating to note how these reactions corresponded with Alvin's reaction when, as a fifteen-year-old, he saw Katherine Dunham's company for the first time. "Their moves, their jumps, their agility, the sensuality of what they did, just blew me away. I was taken into another realm. It was just a transcendent experience for me."

Over the next twenty years, I saw the company dance some

two dozen times, always making sure to see *Revelations*. I also wrote several articles on the company for different publications and got to know Alvin mainly through his work.

In an *Ebony* article focusing on the company's twenty-fifth anniversary celebration in 1984, Alvin couldn't forget problems even while celebrating. "Money is a never-ending problem," he said. "For instance, we had planned, during our anniversary celebration this fall, to make four ballets over a period of two months. We now have been asked to make two ballets over a period of eight months. The situation is very dire. People think that because the company is looking wonderful, everything is fine. They never realize how much all this costs. We still spend more time chasing funds than we do in the studio in creative work."

The harsh reality is that fund-raising was at least partially affected by not-so-subtle attitudes of European supremacy that flow through upper echelons of the dance world. In the *Ebony* article I called it "insidious" that some elements in the dance world and among funding sources "often try to put the company down as being 'too commercial,' deciding it is not possible to be as popular as the Ailey company and still create art."

In the fall of 1987, while visiting friends in New York City, I ran into Alvin on the street. By this time I had moved to Richmond, Virginia. We talked briefly before he invited me to join him in one of his favorite hangouts. It was during this chance encounter that Alvin told me he was considering writing his autobiography. I strongly encouraged him to do it. As a student of men such as Malcolm X, Mahmoud Boutiba, and Harold Cruse, all of whom taught me the importance of information and documentation, I was excited to hear that Alvin, a member of the Dance Hall of Fame, was considering documenting his life and his experiences. After all, his impact on modern dance was no less than that of Jackie Robinson on major league baseball and Thurgood Marshall on the field of law.

From the beginning Alvin was very firm about two things. He wanted his book to be autobiographical, and it was to be called *Revelations*. Some of the company's board members and key staff people were not enthusiastic about his writing his autobiography, he said, but he insisted that this was what he wanted to do and had to do. This book expresses that determination.

Alvin asked me how I thought he should deal in *Revelations* with his famous breakdown, the one that, in 1980, was announced with screaming headlines in New York City newspapers and in quieter articles in papers throughout the country. I suggested that he should look upon the rejection he suffered and the love he lost as a very human thing and that he use the book as an opportunity to tell his side of the story.

In this book, Alvin does just that. For the first time, in *Revelations,* he describes the devastating incident as the culmination of nearly a year of self-destructive behavior. It came close to costing him his sanity.

During our conversation I assumed that Alvin had already chosen the dance writer with whom he would collaborate on the project. Any dance writer would probably seize the opportunity. I certainly did not consider myself a candidate. I had no background in dance, nor did I know Alvin well enough to be considered a friend. I was barely a colleague. Nevertheless, after some time had passed, I told him that I would like to be considered as a collaborator if he hadn't already made his choice. To my surprise, he said he hadn't decided on a writer. He asked whether I thought I could do it from Richmond. "With modern transportation, the telephone, and the fax machine, it would be no problem," I said.

Three or four weeks later, I received a call from Alvin's office: he wanted me to work with him on the project. I exulted in the much-hoped-for invitation.

Alvin never really explained why he chose me over New York City's well-known dance writers, but during our conversations, I began to understand why he might want a black writer. There were things he dealt with in talking about his childhood years that a black writer would probably understand without his having to provide a lot of explanation. There was, for example, the decisive role of music in the lives of black children, especially through the community of the Baptist church. There were also sensitive questions that had plagued Alvin throughout his entire life that required answers from his mother. He had never gotten up the nerve to ask her himself, so he urged me to raise these questions with her and bring him her answers.

The first issue concerned a memory of something he had seen when he was about five years old. His mother had come home very late from work one night, crying, her clothes disheveled. Alvin saw her but didn't make his presence known to her. Later he heard through the grapevine that she had been raped by some white men. All those years he had wanted to know if that was true but hadn't known how to ask her. When I spoke to his mother, Mrs. Lula Cooper, about it, she was surprised to learn that he had seen her that night. Yes, the rape had occurred. I passed the confirmation on to Alvin. He listened but said nothing.

He also wanted to ask her about rumors he had often heard as a child that Alvin Ailey Sr. was not his father. His real father, according to local rumors, was Eddie Warfield. As a child, Alvin had seen Warfield get his face slashed in a fight outside a bar. Mrs. Cooper confirmed that Alvin Ailey Sr., whom Alvin Jr. remembered speaking to only once in his life, was his father. Again I passed her response on to Alvin. Again he listened but said nothing. I believed Alvin needed someone black to deal with this kind of personal information.

Alvin did not find it easy to talk about his private life, especially his childhood. It was only after speaking with Carmen de Lavallade, perhaps his closest friend, that I realized what a breakthrough it was to get him to describe his childhood years in Texas and California. Carmen, for whom he often expressed great affection, knew Alvin from their school days in Los Angeles. In fact, she introduced him to concert dance. She said, "I don't think any of Alvin's personal friends ever really knew him, his background, where he came from, whether he had any family at all. It was only in recent years that we met his mother." That's why she so vividly recalls an incident that occurred during the memorial service for Alvin.

"At his memorial service," she said with a smile, "the pastor got up to talk about Alvin and then got into his childhood. All of a sudden there was this loud noise. It was like somebody had pulled a plug out of the microphone. The pastor was talking, but no one could really hear him. As soon as he stopped talking about Alvin's childhood, the microphone went on again. We all looked at each other and said, 'Did Alvin do that?' I said, 'I bet he did.' After the services were over, everyone was saying, 'Did you hear Alvin pull the plug?' It was so funny. You couldn't feel sad. Everybody had their good cry and everything, but it was just one of those pleasant memories that we'll always talk about. I'm sure Alvin was up there having a grand time laughing at us all." For Carmen and others those are precious memories.

Alvin had his precious memories too, and speaks of them in *Revelations,* but he also had lots of what he called "blood memories, blood memories about Texas, the blues, spirituals, gospel, work songs, all those things going on in Texas in the 1930s during the depression. I have intense feelings about them." Now, for the first time, after having given several hundred interviews in the last thirty years of his public life, he deals with those blood memories.

As Alvin delved into his blood memories, it was obvious that some were more painful than others. This was especially apparent when he talked about his father, Alvin Ailey Sr., with whom he had spoken for about ten minutes during his entire life. That relationship, or to be more accurate, that *lack* of a relationship, the rejection he felt, had a profoundly negative effect on Alvin's life. The rejection was compounded by his name: he was the junior of a man who did not care for him. It must have been hard being a junior when senior was not around. Even his closest friends didn't know he was Alvin Jr. until his death, when Jr. was printed after his name in the program of the memorial service at the insistence of his mother. He asked me about my father and told me how lucky I was to have such a long, continuous, loving relationship with my father, who is eighty-four years old.

During our interview sessions, Alvin was most animated when talking about black music he had heard as a child in church, on the streets, or coming out of the local honky-tonk. It was obvious that he was totally captivated by black music in all of its forms. He got so carried away when talking about the singing of some black women on a street corner in one of the small Texan towns he'd lived in that right on tape he sang a verse of the song he had heard them singing. At other times, Alvin would use expressive body language and facial expressions when recalling a particularly funny incident. Alvin could tell a story verbally as superbly as he could choreographically.

The interviews were always conducted in the Hotel Consulate in Manhattan because Alvin made it clear that, autobiography or no autobiography, meeting at his apartment was out of the question. "Nothing personal," he assured me. "I just don't have people over." During later interviews with his friends and colleagues, I found that people who had known him for twenty years or more had never seen the inside of his various apartments.

It was clear from the beginning that though Alvin was serious about wanting to collaborate on his autobiography, he was not prepared for the hours of interviewing required to successfully complete such a venture. He wanted to do other things. There were times when he was traveling. One trip took him to Italy for several weeks to choreograph a ballet for the La Scala Opera Ballet. At other times, he wanted to hang out at one of his favorite watering holes rather than talk about his life. He also spent several weeks in the hospital. On occasion he would direct me to speak to other people. I told him that was cool, but since he wanted an autobiography, he had to tell his story in his own words. Others could fill in only fragments of his life.

Sometimes we would set aside six to eight hours over a couple of days to work on the book, and I would be lucky if I got three good hours out of the planned six. There were times when he wanted to talk about anything but autobiographical material. That's why we didn't complete all the interviews before he died. But when he was ready, he talked openly and revealingly about his life, his experiences, his beliefs, his creativity, his influences and inspirations, his joys, his feelings, his overpowering obsession with dance, his vision, his pain, his needs, his disappointment, his insufficient self-esteem, his searching, and his fatherless childhood. Alvin didn't get around to everything, but he did tell me enough to guarantee that *Revelations* would more than live. up to its title.

The period from 1954, when Alvin came to New York City, to 1989, when he died, saw many significant political, economic, and cultural changes, both nationally and internationally. Alvin, through his dance, was a contributor to and beneficiary of those changes. *Revelations,* in his own words, will illuminate and document some of the hows and whys of his unique and absorbing life.

$\mathcal{R}$evelations

The Autobiography of Alvin Ailey

ONE

The Texas Years

My first memory of Texas is being glued to my mother's hip as we thrashed through the terrain looking for a place to call home. We never had a place, a house of our own. When I say "thrashed through the terrain," I mean branches slashing against a child's body that is glued to his mother's body as they walk through the mud in bare feet, going from one place to another. I'm talking about Texas mornings when the dew was lost in a hug of nothingness. Where one wants to be someplace and he's not there and there is no father.

I'm talking about living with aunts, cousins, and grandparents and not truly belonging anywhere. My deepest memories are of a place called Rogers, Texas, where my mother and I rented a house with no furniture. There were big trees outside full of devil horses. Devil horses are praying mantises. There was a tree in the front yard completely filled with praying mantises. Once I shook it, causing thousands of them to fall to the ground. I was frightened to death of those things, though they are really harmless.

There was Temple, Texas; Rogers, Texas; and Cameron, Texas. In all those places there were aunts who had big houses with attics, dolls, wonderful food, and wonderful overstuffed couches. In Rogers there were mostly mills, filling stations, and schools. There was a black school, all run down, at the bottom of the hill. At the top was this gleaming castle, the school where the white children went. In Rogers there was also a church where the gospel was preached. It was the center of my community. The church was always very important, very theatrical, very intense. The life that went on there and the music made a great impression on me. At a church in Cameron, when I was about nine, I watched a procession of people, all in white, going down to a lake. The minister was baptizing everybody as the choir sang "Wade in the Water." After baptism we went into church where the minister's wife was singing a soulful version of "I've Been 'Buked, I've Been Scorned." The ladies had fans that they fluttered while talking and singing. All of this is in my ballet *Revelations*.

I lived in Cameron, Texas, for some months with one of my aunts and her children. I remember being in bed with a twelve-year-old cousin when I was eight and rubbing against her warm body. I remember the house being full of aunts, full of love, full of needs and wants. My mother was off working the cotton fields all day. When I was very young, only about four or five, I also picked cotton. After being picked, the cotton was put in big bags and placed on wagons. When I got tired I would go up to the road and watch for snakes. When we left the cotton field at sunset, I would sit on one of the wagons and ride home. I remember the people moving in the twilight back to their little shacks.

After picking cotton all week or otherwise working for white people, black people would get all dressed up on Saturday night and go off to one of the Dew Drop Inns, where Tampa

Red and Big Boy Crudup would be playing funky blues music. Black people were joyful in both church and the Dew Drop Inns in spite of their miserable living conditions.

Texas, during my childhood, was a charter member of the racist South. In the twenty-five years before my birth, some forty-five black men and women were lynched in Texas. Older black people in the mean-spirited, dirt-poor, sparsely populated Brazos Valley, which is located in the southeastern part of the state, used to talk about the racism among themselves, but we kids overheard them.

We were aware that the Ku Klux Klansmen were striking terror in the area even while I was growing up. I saw them more than once dressed in their white robes. A few of the more terrifying headlines that ran in Texas newspapers screamed, "Lots Drawn for Souvenirs of Lynched Negro's Anatomy," "Triple Lynching Follows Thrilling Texas Man Hunt," and "Heart and Genitals Carved From Negro's Corpse." Lynchings occurred in several cities, including Houston, Beaumont, Paris, Waco, Palestine, Newton, Fort Worth, Huntsville, and Navasota, one of the small towns in which my mother and I lived.

When I was about five years old, my mother was raped by four white men. She never admitted to me that it happened. She only recently found out that I knew about it. One night she didn't come home until ten P.M. She usually came home at three or four in the afternoon. She probably had been working in some white people's kitchen. That was the other kind of work, along with picking cotton, available to black people. It was very clear to me that my mother was crying. She had bruises all over her body. I don't think she ever told anyone about it except maybe her sisters or friends from church. I kept quiet and pretended I was asleep the whole time.

In the local movie houses black kids had to sit in the balcony. Sometimes my mother would roast peanuts, and I would sell them outside the movie house. Sometimes when we didn't have food I would eat many of them as well as Texas clay.

In one of the places where we lived—I don't remember which—a Mexican family lived down the road from us. They became my very good friends. There were about six kids in the family. I was closest to Manuel. He and his brothers taught me how to speak Spanish. Manuel and I would run through the fields together, across the railroad tracks by the school over to the white section of town. We'd sit by the highway and watch the trucks pass. There was a small bridge called Little Rock Bridge that spanned the creek. Manuel and I—we were both seven—loved to go there and play. There were big rocks on the bridge on which a number of snakes would curl. They were probably water moccasins. We'd throw small stones at the snakes to force them into the water. Then we would get into the water and muddy it until the snakes came up, gasping for air. Then we'd grab them and throw them up on the bank. None ever bit us. We had a great time messing with the snakes.

After the Mexican family moved away, Chauncey Green became my best friend. He was a rough kid, twelve years old. I was then eight. At the time mother and I were living with Mr. Amos Alexander in Navasota, Texas. He was a wonderful, tall black man who had a big limp. And he was in love with my mother. In back of his house there was an enormous tank for storing water that must have been twenty feet deep. It was also very slick on the edges. When the weather got hot Chauncey and I used to play around the tank to keep cool, despite having been warned repeatedly to stay away from it. Texas is a very hot place. The sun comes up like thunder. It breathes down your back. It seethes. It sears you. On one of those hot days I fell into the tank and almost drowned. Chauncey saved my life. I went under the water three times, thrashing my arms and gasping for air, before Chauncey pulled me out. My mother, thank God, was not home and to this day doesn't know what happened. Chauncey managed to push all the water out of me. As he pushed the water, he also lay on top of me. He thought it was fun to lie on me and make what amounted to sexual movements. I guess I became a kind of sexual object for Chauncey. I didn't mind, but he introduced me to passivity, to being a kind of sexual object of an older guy.

When I was about nine or ten, I became friends with a girl who was about my age. We used to rub up against each other and examine each other with our hands. I had sexual fantasies about her, but Chauncey ended that. He treated me like a girl, and though I didn't want to be treated like a girl, I felt I owed him something. After all, he had saved me from drowning.

The house we lived in with Mr. Alexander had five rooms, two of them bedrooms. My mother and Mr. Alexander had one bedroom; I had the other. The house was on stilts. Under the house I found a nest of snakes. I would take biscuits, syrup, and whatever else I could find and feed them. I got very upset when my mother found me doing this and she went and killed the snakes with a hoe. I didn't think they were dangerous. The idea of feeding snakes is something that still permeates my life.

Mr. Alexander was a kind, sweet man who taught me to ride horses, gave me my first dog, and taught me how to plant fruit and pecan trees. I also had the responsibility of feeding the chickens and hogs, rounding up the cows, and weeding and watering the garden. Many children might have considered these chores a royal pain, but for me, after moving around so much, they represented stability. Mr. Alexander had an old Victrola, the kind with the white dog on top, and lots of records. For the first time I could listen to all the records I wanted to. He also had an old piano. Thus, for many hours I could lose myself in the music that had always enthralled me.

Mother seemed as happy to be with Mr. Alexander as I was.

She finally had a real kitchen to cook in, and the house was full of the heady smells of cornbread, biscuits, collard greens, pies, pork chops, fried chicken, and black-eyed peas. She eventually got a good job in the Navasota Hospital as its first black employee.

Even with our new place to live, Texas was a tough place for a black boy in the 1930s. Race and the economy were both big problems. The depression years were bad, and there were few jobs to be had. But children will always find a way to have fun. I had some of my best times riding my bicycle. Once I rode my bike over to the white section of town and accidentally ran into an elderly white lady, hitting her in the leg. I was scared shitless and biked back to the black section of town as fast as I could pedal. I was old enough to know that I didn't belong on that side of town, which was literally on the other side of the railroad tracks.

The place where the adults had fun was the Dew Drop Inn. Folks got together there on weekends. On Saturday nights I used to go over there to watch the action. I was much too young to go in, so I stood around and looked in the door. For the adult party-goers, it was the place to be. My mother was in there, and everybody was doing what were considered to be nasty dances. The Dew Drop Inn was a rough place. The women wore bright, flashy red dresses. The men wore equally flashy suits. The men also carried big knives called Texas Specials and did a lot of fighting. There was one Dew Drop Inn which was a real honky-tonk out on the road with a little bar, crude furniture, and a blaring jukebox. I would hang around on the outside and watch people fall out of there at three A.M. It was there one night I saw a man named Eddie Warfield get his cheek slashed open— the same Eddie Warfield some people were calling my real father.

Many of the same people who went to the Dew Drop Inn

on Saturday night went to church on Sunday morning. In dance I deal with these two very different worlds. *Blues Suite* is a Dew Drop Inn; *Revelations* is the church.

Another time for fun in those small Texas towns was the arrival of Silas Green from New Orleans, a traveling vaudeville-like show with ladies in sequined bikinis and loud carnival music. Kids weren't allowed in to the late show, the one featuring the ladies, but I'd stay up and sneak away from home and look under the tent. I'd wonder where the men were going with those bikini-clad ladies at two in the morning.

There were also house parties where itinerant musicians would perform and let us know what was happening in the last town they had visited. Musicians like Sonny Boy Williamson, Blind Lemon Jefferson, and Big Boy Crudup were among those who would come to Sunday barbecues and play music while everybody danced. Their singing, and the singing of other people there, affected me a lot. Sometimes maids would stand on street corners and sing "When the Lord get ready, child, you got to move. You may be rich, you may be poor, you may have money or you may have none, but when the Lord God get ready, you got to move."

In many ways those depression years were a time of love, a time of caring, a time when people didn't have much, but they had each other. It was a time that filled me with joy, love, and some anger. Mr. Alexander had a sister who had a son called Junior. I remember sitting out in the Texas twilight sipping iced tea or lemonade with Junior and feeling like I didn't belong. I knew Mr. Alexander loved me and my mother, but when his relatives were there, I felt like they were his family and my mother and I were interlopers. I felt that I was there and yet I was not. In 1961 I made a ballet about that feeling: *Knoxville: Summer of 1915.*

At that time I attended an all-black elementary school

located in the white section of town. There was a railroad track near the school, and I often had to crawl under standing trains to get to my classes. There was also a busy highway that ran by the school, causing loud noises during school hours. We were lucky that most of the teachers tried hard to teach us. The educational methods were very progressive for a poor black school.

I had very little to do with white people as a small child, except in the stores. In the stores sometimes you could try on clothes, sometimes you couldn't. You could certainly buy, because your money was good no matter what your color was. But as far as visiting white neighborhoods or socializing with whites, it wasn't done.

I remember my mother's family, the Cliffs, especially Norman Cliff, her father. He was very pale and lived on a farm outside Temple, Texas. When I was seven or eight, I spent the summer with Granddaddy Cliff, who was then seventy years old. He was quite wonderful. He chewed tobacco and was very good to me.

Mother says that her grandfather, Jenkins Cliff, was a white man from the state of Washington. He was basically a wandering handyman. Somehow he met my great-grandmother, Louisa Cliff—they had the same last names—who lived in Milano, Texas. Mother says they were a striking couple. She was lean, pretty, and very dark-skinned; he was six feet tall and had blond hair and blue eyes. They had six children. Since they couldn't live together legally or otherwise in Texas, he found work in San Antonio and slipped into Milano on Friday nights to see his family. Mother says that on his visits she and the rest of his grandchildren would run and meet him, knowing that he usually had hugs and goodies for them.

My great-uncle, according to Mother, was a stud on the plantation of a man named Ketchum. His major function was to father children on Ketchum's female slaves. I remember meeting

Uncle Dan once as a small child when he was ninety years old. I had no idea of his unusual past until many years later.

I often felt terribly rejected during those early years in Texas. Most of the time my mother was either away working or looking for work, and I didn't understand why she was away so much. Here she was, a twenty-six-year-old woman with a young boy and no place to call home, so it must have been a tough period for her, too. She did some things that were really rough on me and gave me an inferiority complex *forever*. She used to drink a lot, and she would scream and holler and beat me when I cried as she was on her way out the door. To me she was one of the most beautiful women in the world, an extraordinary beauty like Lena Horne in her heyday. I always wanted all her attention and felt neglected when I didn't get it. But then, what woman of twenty-six wants to be saddled with a seven-year-old boy, especially if she's alone? Not only was my mother dragging this child around, but the child, I've heard, was fat and ugly.

There were also quieter times, better times, when Mother and I would take long walks in the woods. I loved those moments because then I had her solely to myself. I wanted them to stretch on and on. She would laugh and play with me and point out each little animal we saw. Often I would pick wildflowers and present them to her with a great flourish.

The depth of my mother's love for me was revealed by an incident when I was very young. In a fit of hunger while she was out, I ate a pile of half-cooked beans she was preparing for dinner. By nightfall, Mother tells me, I was desperately ill, my stomach bloated from eating all those beans. There was no hospital or clinic nearby and no doctor to be called for home visits, so she had to put me on her back and walk eight miles down a dark country road to the nearest doctor. He gave me a heavy dose of castor oil that quickly cleaned my stomach out.

Mother said, "We named you Alvin Ailey Jr. because we

had already decided that you were going to be our only child."
She was concerned about whether I was going to come out of
her dead or alive. "I walked around during the last few months
of my pregnancy scared to death that I was carrying a dead baby
inside me," she told me. "Either that or the laziest baby ever
conceived. You didn't move one time before birth." I told her
that this proved I was smart enough to conserve my energy for
the critical struggle for survival that awaited me in the rough
world outside.

Like most black babies of the Brazos Valley I wasn't born in
a hospital. My entry was made in Grandfather Ailey's home on
January 5, 1931. My delivery room contained a bed for my
mother, a potbellied stove, which provided the only heat that
early, cold morning, and a cot for the doctor. At birth I became
the thirteenth member of an already overcrowded household
that included my parents, my grandfather Henry Ailey, my aunt
Nettie, her eight children, and her son-in-law.

Mother said I was an alert child from the beginning. "Less
than twenty-four hours after you were born, instead of sleeping
like a sensible baby you were checking everything going on
around you. The doctor said you were one of the most curious
babies he had ever seen."

My father was never there. I never knew him; I never saw
him. As a child it seemed that I was the only one without a
father, and that hurt deeply. Chauncey and Manuel had fathers.
Most other children I knew had fathers. But I didn't, and the
man's absence affected me all my life. The inferiority complex
that resulted from being a fatherless child never did go away.

My mother never said anything about his absence or gave
me any explanation of why he wasn't there. I don't think she
liked him at all. I used to imagine that they just got together one
day and she decided to have me.

I have been told that my father was a violent man and that he and his brother used to chase the Ku Klux Klan on horses. He had seven brothers, and they were wild. I used to wonder whether my mother and father were married. She once told me that she was not married to Alvin Ailey Sr., that my father was another man named Eddie Warfield whom she really loved dearly and about whom I've heard relatives speak. Then again, only recently, she declared that Alvin Ailey Sr. really was my father and that they were married when he was eighteen and she was fourteen, despite strong objections from her family.

There was something about the Ailey family that my mother wanted me to stay away from, something about them she didn't like. She never said to me, "Why don't you get to know your father?" He had married again and had two children by his second wife.

I spoke to him for the first and only time in 1975 or 1976. Calling him was something I had been thinking about for years. My desire to get in touch had obvious roots; there was another man somewhere in the world named Alvin Ailey, a man who happened to be my father. I wanted to know what he was, who he was, how he was. How I related. I was looking for a space for myself, looking for some description of why I am the way I am.

I don't remember exactly where I got his telephone number; I think I called a relative in Temple, Texas, to find out where he was. I had to make several calls. At the time, he was working as a janitor in a movie theater in Wichita Falls, Texas. The call lasted maybe ten minutes and lacked real warmth on both sides. It was not "Sonny boy, I love you" or "Daddy, I love you. Why don't we get together?" It was very cold, very matter-of-fact, and he told me nothing about his life. The conversation went something like this. I said, "This is Alvin, your son Alvin Ailey." He said, "Yeah, I've seen your name around in the newspapers. I know you have a dance company and I'd like to see you." I said, "I'd like to see you, too. I want to come and see you." We made a tentative date for me to visit him in Texas. He asked me to send him a poster. After the call I had every intention of going to Texas. But I never did. I never went. Why I didn't go I can no longer recall. Something may have come up with the company; maybe I was frightened about confronting myself. I never sent the poster. I never called him again.

Still, I would periodically have these yearnings to know more about him and about the Ailey side of the family. One time, feeling this urge particularly strongly, I called one of my aunts in Temple. She said, "Boy, your father done died." My father had been a heavy drinker, and cirrhosis of the liver had killed him. He had been buried two or three weeks before my call. Of course, that news brought on feelings of depression. Now there was no way I would ever get to know Alvin Ailey Sr.

I've seen only one picture of my father; it was on his funeral program. Staring at me was a round man with a hat, a man who didn't look much like me. I looked at the picture and tried to find myself in it, the eyes, the nose, any possible resemblance. I wondered how it would be to have been this man. What the feeling would be. What there was of me in him and of him in me.

About three or four years after he died, my mother and I went to Texas and toured the area where we had once lived, all those little towns. During our visit I met my half brother, Lonnie. He was a dapper dresser and one of the biggest pimps in Texas. I spent a night at his roadhouse. It had big brass beds and employed twenty white girls. Sometimes he would drive me uptown in this sharp green Cadillac with some of those white girls in tow. White passersby gave us the strangest looks. Lonnie was often in trouble with the law, and on one occasion I bailed him out of jail.

I also met his mother and my half sister, Nettie Jean. She had a son who wanted to come to the Ailey School, but my mother discouraged this for fear that the boy and I were getting to close.

In later years, mother told me a little more about my father. She described him as "a fine-looking, dark-skinned man with curly hair." They met while attending church in Rogers, Texas. Mother said, "My family was disturbed by both his lack of a job and his seeming disinclination to look for one. I think the only reason they let me marry him was a fear that I might be pregnant. He didn't have the education and get-up-and-go to take care of a family."

According to Mother, he left shortly after I was born, returned briefly when I was about four years old, and then left for good. I have no memory of him as a child, and I feel that the search for the man I never knew came to color my entire life.

TWO

Los Angeles

When Mother and I moved in with Mr. Amos Alexander in Navasota, I thought that at last we had a permanent home, one where I could call a man father. Then, when I was twelve, mother decided that rather than staying with Mr. Alexander, she would move to California, where she could find a job in the aircraft industry. I would stay with Mr. Alexander in Navasota for several months until she got it together. Then she would send for me. So my mother went away in May or April 1941. She found a job, and later I was placed on a train alone for one more move, this time to Los Angeles. The trip took eighteen hours. I was angry with her for moving away from Mr. Alexander.

The year was 1942. The war was on when I arrived in Los Angeles and was met by my mother. I found a city that was completely wrapped up in the war. For a short time we lived on the east side of Los Angeles, which was the black section of town, and then we moved into a big apartment house in a predominantly white area where my mother took a housecleaning job. It was another kind of life in the white section of town. The buildings were bigger; the people had more money. I remember very well seeing my mother on her knees scrubbing these white folks' rooms and halls. That image is in my ballet *Cry*.

This was a very exciting time for me, coming from a southern rural background and having lived in all those little country towns. The idea of everybody living close together was thrilling for me. I was absolutely overjoyed to be part of so much activity, in the midst of all that street life. It was a very good time in a very good, active place. Because of the booming war economy everybody seemed to be doing well.

It seemed that everybody was working for the aircraft industry, especially Lockheed, which was where my mother eventually went to work. When my mother began working there, as one of the first black "Rosie the Riveters" on the midnight shift, it seemed she was never at home. She would leave for work at midnight and return home around nine or ten o'clock in the morning. She used to leave me twenty-five cents a day for lunch. She slept all day while I was at school and then was gone by the time I got home.

Ophelia Wilkes, a next-door neighbor, used to look after me. She was a tall black woman with long legs, long arms, and no hair; Judith Jamison looks exactly like her. A wonderful woman, a very warm woman. She'd see to it that I got to bed when my mother went to her job.

Ophelia had a boyfriend named Campbell who worked as a porter with the railroad. In our neighborhood that made him wealthy. One day I came home from school and found policemen and an ambulance in front of the house. And there, at the top of this outdoor stairway, stood Ophelia, looking like Electra, a tall black woman in a black dress. I heard her say defiantly and full of rage. "Yes, I shot the yellow motherfucker." She had shot Campbell in the leg because she thought he had another girlfriend. (She got no time.) Ophelia, too, is in my ballet *Cry*.

When Ophelia moved away, another family moved in. They had a daughter who tried to teach me to play the piano. Her family was devoutly religious, so just as I was learning Rachmaninoff I was being told about the glory of Jesus.

For a short time, I went to an all-white school on the west side. I hated it. I just couldn't relate to those people, and the whole month I spent there was a miserable one. I think it was because of my misery that my mother moved back to the east side of town. We took an apartment on East Forty-third Place, which is where I lived for a number of years. The schools were not integrated in those days, and there was a strong division of where you could go to school. Soon after I moved there and started going to mostly black McKinley Junior High School, the name was changed to George Washington Carver Junior High School. In those days black people were forced into certain sections of town; the lines were drawn on where you could live. You couldn't buy a house or get an apartment in other sections of town, so you had to go to schools that were essentially segregated.

George Washington Carver Junior High School was a wonderful experience for me. I made many good friends there, especially Kiyoshi Mikawa, a Japanese. Kiyoshi was a genius at mathematics, a subject that baffled me; he used to help me with my math all the time. Tony Hernandez, a Spanish kid, was another close friend. The idea of a multiracial world was always there in spirit, even when I was very young. I was part of it.

I lived right around the corner from school, so my friends and I would go to my home to eat lunch. I was aware that the government was forcing Japanese families into internment camps during the war. I don't know why Kiyoshi's family wasn't moved into one; maybe they were later, but I have no recollection of it.

I found Los Angeles fascinating. I discovered Central Avenue. It has gone to pot now, but in those days it was full of clubs, and movie and vaudeville theaters. There was one movie theater very close to where I lived, on Forty-third and Central, named after the dancer Bill Robinson. That's where my friends and I went to the movies every Friday. A little farther down the street was a tiny movie theater called the Rosebud, which was very glamorous, with neon lighting. Even farther down, and more important to me, was the Lincoln, a vaudeville theater that presented movies and live shows. It was a big movie palace like all the classical prewar movie palaces. It was there I saw Pigmeat Markham doing his "Here Come de Judge" sketches. Lena Horne made a guest appearance once. They had a chorus line of gorgeous girls; they had strippers; they had bands. I saw Duke Ellington there for the first time.

The Lincoln was a remarkable place and had a marked influence on me. Though I was only thirteen, I had no problem getting in. All you had to have was the money, and admission was only fifty cents, so the theater became my haunt. My friends and I would roam through the balconies of this great place during the movie, waiting for the vaudeville sketches to come on. I was very impressed with Pigmeat Markham, who did racy sketches with a group of gorgeous chorus girls clad in scanty costumes. I was absolutely bowled over by the glitter and the glitz of Lincoln Theater.

I was also very impressed with Lucky Millinder and all the black entertainers who haunted the Lincoln. As I came to realize years later, it was like the Apollo Theater in Harlem, full of the best black entertainment. It was the place to go, except on Friday nights, when we went to the Bill Robinson Theater.

There was also a nightclub called the Club Alabama, with all sorts of singers and entertainers. One singer—I can no longer recall her name—was called Little Miss Cornshucks. We loved her, but we couldn't get in the club because of our ages. So we'd go by there at night and put our ears to the door so we could hear Little Miss Cornshucks. She looked like a doll with her blond wig, striped stockings, and big shoes. Jimmy Truitte (I didn't know him at the time) danced there as a chorus boy. In those days the chorus boys and chorus girls were all light-skinned.

I was very much into reading in high school and college. Mathematics was never my strong suit, but I loved literature, especially the classics. In studying Spanish literature while at UCLA, I discovered the South Americans—poets and writers like Pablo Neruda, Octavio Paz, and Rubén Darío. I found a lot of spiritual uplift in their work. While I was studying French, Baudelaire became a great favorite of mine. Among black writers I discovered John Oliver Killens, Richard Wright, and Chester Himes. I found their work very racy and sexy. I was also taken by poets like Countee Cullen. Langston Hughes didn't come on until much later. I was also fond of Tennessee Williams. One of my first ballets was based on themes from Tennessee Williams's plays.

My affinity for languages began in Texas when I ran around with Manuel and his brothers. They would speak to me in Spanish, and I learned to respond in Spanish. In junior high school I took Spanish classes. Later, in high school, I studied French. I never learned to speak it fluently, but I can understand it. I also speak a little Italian. My Spanish was so good in high school that teachers would let me teach the class sometimes.

In junior high school I had a teacher named Mildred Cobbledick, a white lady who would sit on a stool with all of her legs showing. She introduced me to Gilbert and Sullivan's *Mikado* and other kinds of choral music. I fell in love with *The Mikado* and would get up and sing its music as soon as the teacher left the room.

I also did a little dancing in the backyard of our house. I saw many Gene Kelly and Fred Astaire movies, and the idea came to me that moving around could express all that was inside you. I started collecting records. I would dance to the music. Transistors didn't exist then, so I couldn't take the phonograph out to the yard, but I would bounce around on the grass making up steps. I would imitate Gene Kelly and, after I saw *Stormy Weather,* the Nicholas Brothers. Though I was impressed by the Nicholas Brothers and it became the vogue for everybody in the neighborhood to do tap dancing, I didn't want to be a tap dancer. Even so, I took lessons in tap from a lady named Loretta Butler. My mother took me downtown and bought me a pair of tap shoes. I think I went to three lessons, learning the time step on a very slick living-room floor. This huge lady would beat out the time with a little stick. I couldn't stay with that; it just wasn't me.

In junior high school and high school, I had no idea of becoming a dancer—no feeling or desire for it at all. Men didn't dance; you were a sissy (*sissy* was a big word back then) if you danced. You couldn't even *think* about dancing. When I first saw Carmen de Lavallade dance in high school, she danced alone. The guy who choreographed for her was a terrific dancer, but he didn't dance. So I had all that working against me. But even if I managed to overcome all the obstacles to a dance career, there were few places for a black man to be a dancer in the early 1940s. It was later in the 1940s that I saw the Dunham Company and other dance troupes and began to change my way of thinking.

My mother married Fred W. Cooper, a navy man, when I was fourteen. He became a member of the household and apparently adored me because of my mother. I couldn't stand him at first because I thought he was demanding and getting all my mother's attention. We lived in this little second-floor apartment; they had a bedroom, and I had a little room and slept on a cot. I would sometimes sit at the kitchen table and write poems until three or four o'clock in the morning. (I wanted to be a writer, so I wrote a lot of poetry when I was in high school.) As I sat there trying to write I could hear my mother and Fred carrying on in the room next door. To get away from their sexual activities I would go to the roof, or else I would sit on the front porch or wander up and down the streets for several hours and sneak back in by climbing up on the roof or garage and back to my room to sleep.

I had some artistic friends and some who were not. I knew most of the gay people in junior high school and high school. I had no qualms about being with one kid named Robert. Robert was artistically inclined. He wanted to be pretty and would apply my mother's favorite powder, a little nut-brown powder. He also processed his hair. He had dreams of becoming a fashion designer in Hollywood and painted ties for himself.

I had a lot of homosexual fantasies before I ever got into doing anything actually physical. Once, when I was fifteen, I dressed in drag. There was a Halloween party going on across the street, and something possessed me. My mother was at work, and I went home, dressed in her clothes, and returned to the party in makeup, high-heeled shoes—the works. And yet I can honestly say that at that stage of my life I had no idea what was happening.

I also used to run the streets with a gang of boys. There were four or five of us, and there was one guy, an older man, the other guys had sex with. He would give them beer and money, but I stayed out of that.

My friends and I would wrestle on people's lawns. I had warm feelings toward them, but they were headed in a direction I didn't want to follow. It reached a point where I had to choose between the criminal and the artistic, and my feeling for light, images, movement, and music was growing.

When the boys I ran around with decided to rob a store, they asked me to go with them. I remember taking ten minutes to find the courage to say no. It was a turning point; I knew that I had made a moral decision—lonely but right. I didn't want to go to jail; I didn't want to rob anybody or do anything vicious to another person. So I went home. They did rob the store, and later some of them were imprisoned. Some are still in prison.

After graduating from junior high school I entered Jefferson High School. It, too, was a segregated school, eighty-five percent black and the rest Latino. This was a whole new world for me. Everybody was more mature, and the studies were more exacting. The library was bigger; the sports were more important and professional. Everything was enlarged in high school; there were more things to do, and I enjoyed that a lot. Since I was big for my age, a gym teacher named Bruce Taylor, a man with a stub of an arm, insisted that I should be on the football team. He was a tough cookie. He made me a right tackle. That lasted about two weeks. I said, "Coach, you know these people running and knocking me down and me running after them isn't going to get it. This just isn't going to work." "What's wrong with you," he said, "you some kind of sissy?" I wanted to say yes, but I couldn't do it. What I did instead was change from football to track. I stayed with the team for about ten days but then gave that up, too. I couldn't run the hundred meters in twenty seconds or do the mile in ten minutes. I felt defeated by my total failure at competitive sports.

I ended up doing gymnastics. It's a solo sport, and nobody was trying to get me to go against Jimmy next door or the rest of the school. Gymnastics fitted right in with the dancing I had been doing in the yard. I did the rings and several gymnastic activities, but doing free floor exercise was what really turned me on. The movement of the body was similar to dance. I remember watching other gymnasts do their thing and saying to myself, "That's me." Dancing is like gymnastics, a solo art. When I started dancing, I danced by myself. I always maintained that I created a company so I could dance and do what I wanted to do.

The teachers in high school were very good about taking us places, and I began to learn more about Los Angeles. Once we all went to a radio station and saw Lena Horne. She was about twenty-five years old then—and what a gorgeous creature she was! We couldn't close our mouths we were so awestruck. I got her autograph on a little yellow piece of paper, and I have it still.

Another teacher, a social science teacher whose name I can no longer recall, took us to the ballet at the Los Angeles Philharmonic Auditorium. I had never been in downtown Los Angeles. It was a whole new world to me. I was completely freaked out by all the colorful people, all the huge, luxurious stores, all the glittering theaters and their flashy neon signs. I saw *Scheherazade* with all the costumes, all the fifty million people. I was completely blown away by the live orchestra. The only orchestra I had ever heard was a little jazz band, the Lucky Millinder Band, with sixteen pieces. But to hear a fifty-piece orchestra, to be way up there and look down on such a spectacle, was an unforgettable experience. I left the theater walking on air, totally enchanted. I couldn't believe what I had seen, what I had heard. I couldn't wait to go back again.

The class had attended a two o'clock matinee, and now that I knew where the theater district was, it became my habit to go downtown in time for the matinee and then wander around the theater district afterward to take in all the activity. Whatever show or act or musical event was happening, I would go, whether I knew what it was or not. I discovered the Orpheum Theater, where all the big bands appeared. I saw Tommy Dorsey, Art Tatum, all the biggest jazz artists. In the late 1940s, Los

Angeles was a haven for musicians and singers.

I also discovered the Biltmore, a small legitimate theater. I saw several plays and revues there. I got the chance to see Mae West in the flesh. I also saw lots of musicals at the Los Angeles Philharmonic Auditorium. For one season I saw everything that came along. Edward Lester was producing these musicals. I saw *The Red Mill, The Chocolate Soldier, Naughty Marietta,* and, most important, *Magdelena,* choreographed by a guy named Jack Cole. It really astounded me. The dancing, the color, the light, the movement—especially the movement—had a quality that I had never seen before. I never forgot the man's name, and some of those movements were burned into my memory. I went home immediately and decided I would have to try some of this strange new way of moving.

One day I saw a big poster at the Biltmore featuring Katherine Dunham and her singers, dancers, and musicians. A black woman! I couldn't believe my eyes. A black woman with many black men in wonderful costumes. I was astounded.

I waited impatiently. Finally, the Katherine Dunham Company arrived. Suddenly in front of me, in the flesh, was this unbelievable creature, Katherine Dunham. At the time she was about thirty-one or thirty-two years old. Her singers, dancers, and musicians wore the most glorious costumes; the scenery and the orchestra were just wonderful. She herself came out in the most ravishing costumes and danced and sang with unimaginable precision and beauty. Her beauty was like that of my mother and Carmen de Lavallade combined. Seeing Miss Dunham and her company was a transcendent experience for me.

And the male dancers! Miss Dunham had a group of male dancers, probably fifteen of them, and they were superb. Their moves, their jumps, their agility, the sensuality of what they did, were amazing. I was lifted up into another realm. I couldn't believe there were black people on a legitimate stage in downtown Los Angeles, before largely white audiences, being appreciated for their artistry.

What Miss Dunham was doing was Afro-Caribbean. It was blues; it was spirituals; it touched something of the Texas in me. Her troupe danced in an elegant, exciting, stimulating style that made truthful statements about our culture. They performed at the Biltmore for three weeks. I used to hang around the stage door hoping for a glimpse of some of the dancers. Lucille Ellis, who lives today in Chicago and is a good friend, was one of Miss Dunham's lead dancers. One day she came out and asked, "Boy, what are you doing out here?" I shrugged and said, "You know." She asked, "Have you seen the show?" "Yes," I said. She said, "You need to see it again." So she arranged for the doorman to let me in and show me how to get into the house when it wasn't filled. As a result, in three weeks I saw the Dunham show about eight times.

As I said, I went to matinees, and when my mother didn't know where I was—and she never did—I went in the evenings also. I was thrilled by the magic of Katherine Dunham. Sometimes Lucille would take me downstairs where everybody was busy ironing their skirts and painting their shoes. Every now and then I would pass by Miss Dunham's room, hoping to see her. She had candy-colored wallpaper and red rugs on the floor. Legend had it that every sponsor had to decorate Miss Dunham's dressing room to her specifications; otherwise she would not appear. I think that's apocryphal. I also think it's just wonderful. As I have learned in my life, some dressing rooms are terrible.

At the time, I still didn't consider dance as a career. I wanted to be a teacher of foreign languages or a preacher. I loved preachers. I thought it was the height of power and meaning to get up in front of a congregation in a wonderful costume and talk about fire and brimstone, making everybody sweat. Standing in front of the choir, I thought, was very theatrical, very exciting. But I never thought of myself as a theatrical person—not, that is, until I got to know Carmen de Lavallade.

THREE

Carmen Introduces Me
to Dance

*A*t a school assembly, this beautiful, honey-colored creature in a pink leotard, pink skirt, and pink shoes did a dance to music by Mozart. From the moment I first saw her I was just in a state of pure awe. Anybody who could move around on her toes like that was capable of performing miracles. Her name was Carmen de Lavallade.

I made it my business to find out where Carmen's classes were and arranged to put myself outside every room she was coming out of. Carmen had a sister, Yvonne, who was just as beautiful as she was. Her family is Creole, so she had beautiful light skin, almond eyes, long dark hair, and an infectious, wonderful smile. Carmen's aunt, Miss Adele, owned a bookstore that specialized in books on black history. This was an exotic and daring vocation in the Los Angeles of the 1940s and led some people to call her left-wing. That may be no problem today, but in those days it could get you in trouble with the government, which didn't seem to bother Miss Adele at all.

Carmen and I slowly became friends. She lived in my neighborhood, and I would wait until she and Yvonne passed by my house and then walk behind them to school. On Central Avenue there were all kinds of characters. Yvonne and Carmen, both ravishing creatures, would walk by, and guys would say, "Um! Um! Um! Lunchtime." They would walk a little faster, with their fine selves, and go on to school. They were very shy.

One day a young choreographer in the school picked Carmen to dance the ballet *Scheherazade* for a school assembly. She was dressed in red and looked extremely beautiful. She blew the whole student body away with the combination of her looks and extraordinary dancing. That really did it—I was more in love than ever, and Carmen and I became close friends. I remember fantasizing about dancing onstage with her, but that was impossible. No boy who put any value on his reputation dared dance the way she did and move to that kind of music. He would immediately be branded a sissy. Even those who were clearly sissies didn't have the nerve to try it. When Carmen danced, she danced alone. Though the boy who choreographed *Scheherazade* was a terrific dancer, he wouldn't dance with her. Even he was afraid of being stereotyped.

One day Carmen saw me doing gymnastics and said, "Why don't you come out to where I'm studying?" I asked where the place was. It was "way out in Hollywood," she said. "A man named Lester Horton has a dance studio out there. You should come out and watch the classes." "Sure, why not?" I said.

Another friend, a fellow named Ted who lived around the corner from me, had already told me about Lester Horton. Somehow Ted had found his way out to Horton's studio. He showed me some steps he learned from Lester Horton—strange movements that thrilled me, movements with the torso falling forward. They were incredibly expressive. "What in the world are you doing?" I asked him. He said, "That's exercise number one and exercise number three." And he mentioned Lester Horton's name. So when Carmen also sang Lester Horton's praises, I was persuaded.

Lester Horton's studio was located on Melrose Avenue in Hollywood, a long way from the district where Carmen and I lived. It took us an hour and a half to get there by bus. It was like going from Harlem to Lincoln Center, only we were farther away from his studio than Harlem is from Lincoln Center. The studio was fantastic. Its exterior was painted a kind of chocolate brown; there were two windows with mobiles inside (and I was fascinated by mobiles). The Lester Horton Dance Theater was written across the top in yellow against that brown. The studio held two hundred seats, all painted different colors, and the minute you walked in, you knew you were in the presence of an artistic force.

I sat way off in a corner while Lester Horton taught a class onstage. Lester was a white man from Indiana. He stood about five feet ten and had a short, gray, butch haircut and a very kind face. He was at that time about forty-three. I noticed a small studio in back as well as a space for storing scenery props. There was also a room full of fabrics and costumes and a big room where everyone did makeup.

There was an enormous rack of drums of all shapes and sizes. Lester was teaching class with a drum, not a piano. I couldn't believe what the students were doing onstage. He had stylized a wide range of emotions and a series of strange physical movements into a technique, and everybody, Carmen included, was basically doing it—doing strange turns, falling on the floor, jumping out into space. It had a feeling, an essence, that for me matched something very basic in my makeup. I was thrilled; I couldn't believe what I was seeing. After her class, Carmen and I took the bus home. She attended three classes a week, and for a month I went back with her and watched.

I'll never forget when Lester first put Carmen and me together. Carmen was his leading dancer, and I was your basic country bumpkin. After I had been joined in three or four classes, Lester said, "I want you to rehearse with Carmen." I said, "For what?" "Just do it," he said. When he put us together, the combination was electric. The minute we hit the stage together, it was all there—the lyricism, the emotion, the beauty, and the passion Carmen could express in her dancing. She was like a great actress. Later, on our first tour to Southeast Asia, we did *Roots of the Blues,* a fourteen-minute duet. I would get off the bus moaning about how tired I was. "Ah, I can't do this anymore. I'm too tired." And then I would walk onto the stage with Carmen, and she was already *there;* she was into this dance with you. You'd have to get your steps together because Carmen didn't play on the stage.

Over the years we have come to share many precious memories. We've danced together; we've toured together; we've suffered through the deaths of friends together; we've experienced success together; we've collaborated on several projects; we've taken long walks together; we left the Lester Horton Dance Theater together; we made our Broadway debut together in *House of Flowers.*

Carmen and I went on to dance together many times. *Roots of the Blues* is one of our favorite ballets, maybe because it came directly out of my Texas background. It's about two Southerners all dressed up on a Saturday night with no place to go. They're stuck in their small town, and they sit and watch the trains going through their town to and from Chicago. As a boy growing up in Texas the sounds of trains as they sped by always intrigued me, and the sound of their whistles stayed with me forever.

When Carmen and I danced *Roots of the Blues* at the Boston

Arts Festival in 1961, we left the audience screaming for more. We were told that the mouth of Walter Terry, the famous critic of the *New York Herald Tribune,* literally dropped open when he saw us dance in rehearsal.

Carmen loves *Roots* and constantly reminds me that it should be revived. Over the years, she has been a favorite of choreographers because, in her own words, "I'm someone who's easy to mold." Whatever you want her to dance, she will find a way to do it. Choreographers also love her because she has solid technique and a brilliant, unsurpassable talent for interpreting a ballet.

Carmen encouraged, inspired, and supported me when I first started dancing, when I formed my dance company, when I was hospitalized after a ten-month-long self-destructive fling, when I celebrated several significant anniversaries, when I received various awards of recognition, when I was depressed because of never-ending confrontations with funding sources, and when I was happy about the artistic success of a new ballet. Dance, for me, would have been impossible without Carmen de Lavallade.

.

FOUR

Tentatively Entering the World of Dance

$\mathscr{A}$fter finishing high school I got a job as an office clerk, working for a white guy, Philip Douglas, whom I had met on the beach. He was head of the Atomic Energy Commission's office in Los Angeles. My plan was to work from September until January and save money so I could attend UCLA in February.

I also decided to commit myself to Lester Horton on a regular basis. Classes were twelve dollars a month. I went out there in my sweatpants—tights were beyond consideration in those macho days—and in the back studio I had my first class with Lester himself. He devoted a lot of class time to me, and he was a great teacher. He taught corrective classes, constructed around the needs of the members of the class, what they needed to know, what they needed to do with their bodies. I remember doing exercises against the wall, strange things, stretched out this way, that, and the other. He worked on my feet a lot, which are not the best. And then, after the month was up, I left for UCLA. Lester telephoned me at my house and said, "I think you have something, Alvin. You should come back and work with us. I can put you on work-study. In exchange for classes, you'll work with the stage crew on weekends." The Horton Company had classes all week and performances on Friday and Saturday nights. So I went to UCLA all day and then ran over to the Horton Theater. It was a heavy routine to go to UCLA, then to the Horton Theater, then home, since I had to travel great distances on buses. I was getting up at six o'clock in the morning, taking a two-hour bus ride to UCLA, attending classes until three o'-clock in the afternoon, and taking an hour-long bus ride to the Horton Studio, where I took classes and worked with the stage crew. Lester was preparing a new production.

I still had an enormous conflict in my young mind about what I wanted to do with myself. The beauty, the texture, the paintings, the colors, the people of dance, especially the extraordinary people around the Horton studio, attracted me. But I was convinced there was no future for a black man in dance. Another problem was that the people in Lester's company usually didn't make money. Lester himself lost a lot of money; he acted in a lot of schmaltzy movies to pay for the school. I didn't know that at the time, however; he kept financial matters from us. Everything was just divine so far as we were concerned.

Some of the guys in the Horton Company danced in the same movies that Lester did. It was always a great day when somebody got a job. Some of the dancers lived in the studio because they couldn't afford to rent a room. Theirs was a labor of love. I met some fantastic people there, including Rudi Gernreich, who turned out to be a great clothing designer; Bella Lewitzky, who was Lester's partner and protégé; Bill Bowne, who was Lester's lover; and Constance Finch, whose husband was a brilliant painter. Marge Berman, who is currently teaching at my school in New York City, was one of my first instructors at the Horton School. There was also soap opera star James Mitchell, costume designer Les Brown, and dance professor Larry Warren, the author of Lester's biography, *Lester Horton: Modern Dance Pioneer.* A black girl named Alibe Copage was a part of a black group that included Ray Carrington, Don Martin, and James Truitte. Frank Eng, a Chinese fellow who was a critic for the *Los Angeles Daily News,* came to critique Lester's show and not only fell in love with it but with Lester. Later, he became Lester's general manager.

In the 1940s and 1950s the American dance world practiced a pervasive racism. For a variety of reasons: Our feet weren't shaped right, our butts were too big, our legs wouldn't turn out correctly; blacks simply weren't wanted; and so on. The people who ran the major and minor ballet and modern dance companies coldly rejected, and broke the hearts of, many aspiring young black dancers. In the dance world, at that time, we were not welcome. The white ballet companies didn't want us; neither did the modern dance groups, with the exception of Lester and Martha Graham. Lester—a happy exception—opened his arms to talent when and where he saw it.

I remember a case in point: Janet Collins, Carmen's cousin, made herself a dancer by sheer willpower. Those were the days when they told you, "Your hips are wrong, your back is wrong, your feet are wrong, your legs won't turn out, so don't come to our ballet school." But Janet went there anyway and developed a refined ballet technique. She mostly trained herself and put together a concert, which she performed in Lester's theater. It was from Janet Collins that we got the idea that Lester was open to people of all races. She was a fantastic artist. We put on a ballet of hers in 1971. But she had psychological problems that later drove her to religious extremes and out of the dance world.

There were no press releases sent out praising Lester for

being the pioneer that he was. He did what he did because for him it was the natural thing to do. What it came down to was that, for Lester, his art was much more important than the color of a dancer's skin. That's still a revolutionary notion among those who control dance in this country. Not only did Lester have black people working on the stage crew and taking classes, but he put them in his company. That caused quite a stir. The first performances of Lester's that I saw startled me as much as Katherine Dunham's had, and one of them, *Barrel House*, influenced my very being. *Barrel House* is a blues place where people come to let out their frustrations. The extremely stylized dance featured Bella Lewitzky, Rudi Gernreich, and Herman Bowden. It was an angry rage of a dance, with people in a kind of enclosed, or isolated, state of being. It was a powerful influence on my ballet *Blues Suite*.

Lester was an Indian specialist. He had fallen in love with American Indian culture when he was very young. One of his dances, *Totem Incantation*, was based on a northern Indian ritual. Its lead dancer was Carol Radcliffe, who has a company today in Atlanta. One of the startling effects I remember was scenery with a hole in it; everybody backed up into this hole and disappeared. It was quite wonderful.

Then there was his classic piece *Salome*. He kept working it, presenting a new version every year. Bella Lewitzky was his main dancer, and every year he would make a new version for her. It's about a man who kills his wife out of jealousy, a theme rich in potential conflict and drama. It was not, however, a commercial piece.

I leaned very heavily toward going to Lester, but at the same time, something in me kept saying, "You'd better get an education." There was also that pull at home for me to go to college. I was still so confused by my conflicts about dance that I decided to leave Los Angeles and go to San Francisco. I had always wanted to see it anyway. I thought, "Well, now is the time to go. I'm always at the Horton Studio; I don't have time to study; I've got to get out of here."

I had no money, so to get to San Francisco I borrowed fifty dollars from a good friend. Once there, I lived in various hotels in the black district, the cheapest I could find. I was immediately taken by the beauty of the city—the hills, the water. There was a kind of freedom of attitude that was missing in Los Angeles. I stayed at the YMCA for about a month. I went hungry while looking for a job. The money my friend had lent me ran out during my job hunt.

Finally, I got a state job as a clerk at the tax bureau. I hated the whole idea of taking out files and putting them back, looking through them for numbers. It drove me completely out of my mind. In order to pay the tuition when I started taking courses at San Francisco State College, I took a job with the Greyhound Bus Company. This job, loading bags in and out of buses, was more to my liking, more physical, and it meshed well with my schedule. My shift was from four o'clock till twelve midnight. Then I went to school at eight in the morning.

Although ostensibly I had moved to San Francisco to get away from dance, I knew who the modern dancers were. Soon I found myself attending the Halprin Lathrope Dance Studio. There I met a marvelous girl named Ruth Beckford. I also met Marguerite Angelos, a tall, skinny black girl. Marguerite and I were kindred spirits and decided we should become a dance team. Only twenty-two, she was married to a trumpeter and had a little baby. We would get together on weekends and push her furniture off to the side. For a month or so we rehearsed our routine, with both of us making up the steps. That was the first time I had ever attempted any kind of choreography. She was quite a stimulus—twenty-two years old and striking, with long arms and a long neck. Marguerite—who, as Maya Angelou, would one day become one of America's most famous poets and a role model for women of all colors—could do the most extraordinary moves. I spent more time watching her than I did doing choreography. She was my first partner, but we never danced anywhere outside her apartment. Soon, as so often happens with the young, there were other jobs, new opportunities, and we drifted apart.

One day on Fillmore Street, which is the center of San Francisco, I ran into Lou Fontaine, a choreographer from Los Angeles. He knew that I had studied dancing at Lester Horton's, and he said to me: "I'm doing a show at a place called the Champagne Supper Club tonight. It's the biggest black nightclub in the black area, and I don't have any boys. Why don't you come and be in it? I'll make this dance for you. It will be much better money than working at Greyhound, and you can still go to school."

I thought about it for about three minutes before quitting Greyhound. I performed the dance that Lou choreographed. There was a woman working in Fontaine's group, Miss Hardaway, who was, besides my mother, Carmen, and Miss Dunham, the most beautiful woman I had ever seen. She was a shake dancer who would slowly take off all her clothes. She had sheer net over her entire body, with little patches of material in strategic places. She would walk around, and everybody would scream. An extraordinary performance.

Fontaine had a tap dancer named Teddy Hall whose feet looked almost feathery as he glided across the floor. There was also a group of five or six chorus girls whom I got to know very well. We had a dressing room about as big as a luxury hotel's bathroom, and we all dressed together there. In my role I was some sort of Indian figure in a big war bonnet. Miss Hardaway had a stone in her navel, so I put a stone in mine and applied as much makeup as I could before we went on. We did shows at ten-thirty in the evening and two-thirty in the morning. I hung out a lot with the chorus girls after the last show. There were all kinds of mad parties, with plenty to eat and drink, where the girls, dressed in next to nothing, would parade around in front of the musicians. We would party until four or five o'clock in the morning. I had a lot of wonderful times with them.

Apparently the show we did was very good because we were invited to do a benefit in Los Angeles. Mr. Mosby, who owned the club in San Francisco as well as the one in Los Angeles, gave us permission to do our show down there. We all piled into a bus or station wagons and traveled down to Los Angeles. We did one performance, and as soon as it was over, I went straight to the Horton Studio. I couldn't wait to get there. In the short time that had passed since I'd left for San Francisco, many of the black people were not only taking classes but also dancing, including Jimmy Truitte, Ray Carrington, and Alibe Copage. Lester had choreographed a new ballet called *Yurima*. He had also done *A Touch of Klee,* based on the art of Paul Klee, as well as Duke Ellington's *Liberian Suite,* with Carmen in it. The latter was simply extraordinary. Lester had done any number of very creative new things, and I just sat there, stunned and happy. He was very sweet to me. "Where have you been?" he asked me. "How is school?" And suddenly I knew what I had to do; the die was cast. After having gone through a lot of changes about dance, I made the decision: I would dance. It had taken me four years—from the age of eighteen, when I first got involved with dance and dabbled in it, until twenty-two—to make the decision. For a long time I told myself that I would stick with school and become a language teacher. But after having given school a chance, I knew that I didn't want to spend my life in libraries trying to decipher old Spanish literature; I knew that something athletic was much more interesting and fulfilling for me. Once I had decided, I went back to Lester Horton and said, "Well, here I am."

Mrs. Lula Elizabeth Cooper,
Alvin's mother, in her twenties.
(Courtesy of Mrs. Cooper)

Alvin, eight, with Mrs.
Cooper, whom he considered
"one of the most beautiful
women in the world."
(Courtesy of Mrs. Cooper)

Alvin *(circled)* with classmates at George Washington Carver Junior High School in Los Angeles. *(Courtesy of Mrs. Cooper)*

Alvin, twelve, with Mrs. Cooper *(on his right)* and her friends, Daisy Heard *(left)* and Ellen Heard.
(Courtesy of Mrs. Cooper)

Alvin at fourteen, with Fred Cooper, his stepfather.
(Courtesy of Mrs. Cooper)

Lester Horton, Alvin's first dance instructor and a lifelong influence. *(Courtesy of Marjorie Berman Perces)*

Alvin in costume as a Chinese soldier in the play *The Carefree Tree*, in 1955. He sent the photograph to his mother and wrote on the back: "Recognize me? I look like Fu Manchu." *(Courtesy of Mrs. Cooper)*

Carmen de Lavallade, Alvin's longtime friend, when she was in high school and studying dance with Lester Horton. She introduced Alvin to concert dance. *(Courtesy of Earl Grant)*

Jimmy Truitte was a principal dancer with Lester Horton's company when Alvin studied there in the early 1950s. *(Courtesy of Earl Grant)*

Alvin as a young dancer and actor in New York City in the late 1950s.
(Courtesy of Mrs. Cooper)

FIVE

Hooking Up With Lester

*U*pon my return to the Horton Company in 1953, I began working in earnest. Sometimes the other dancers and I would come into the theater and Lester might be fixing up the wiring. We would say, "What are we going to do today?" and he would answer, "We're going to rewire all the lights," and we would get a lesson in lighting from him. He would talk to us while we were busy helping out, always explaining and teaching. Sometimes we would go out to the scene dock and he would teach us techniques for dyeing scenery panels and fabrics that he'd saved over the years and stored in boxes. Working with Lester was a complete education. Once a month we painted the theater. We would change the colors of the seats or the proscenium, and when we had breaks, we would take down all the Indonesian instruments, and the American Indian instruments and masks, and play and perform. There was music all the time.

When I later choreographed *Knoxville: Summer of 1915*, it was set to a piece of music by Samuel Barber, one of my favorite composers. Lester used to play the piece when we were making costumes or painting sets and scenery. *Knoxville,* so autobiographical at heart, talks about a boy wandering among his family, he not knowing who he is and the family not recognizing him. In the ballet the family is sitting in the front yard in the twilight with this child who wanders among them. This was all about Texas, Mr. Amos Alexander, my mother, Ruby Alexander, and my feeling that they had no notion who I was. Which is a perfect description of how I felt in my youth.

Lester conducted a workshop at the Horton Company in which I did my first choreography. It was based on *Afternoon of a Faun,* which I had seen performed by the Ballet Russe de Monte Carlo on one of my junior high school trips. I made a jazzy version of *Afternoon of a Faun* under Lester's supervision.

There were all kinds of musical influences at the Horton Theater. Lester's taste was eclectic: he loved jazz, blues, American Indian music, and Asian music. He gave us a thorough education not only in dance but in many musical forms. And his influence went beyond the studio. He had a house in Hollywood Hills and would take us there and cook for us. He was an active and adventureous cook, too. He would make a soup based on a Navajo receipe, explaining as he went along both the ingredients of the soup and something about Navajo history. It was always a wonderful education. If there was an occasion for celebration, such as an opening, Lester took the whole company to a restaurant, a different one each time. He introduced us to sushi and tempura and other delights at a Japanese restaurant, then to Mexican food and many other cuisines. He had accounts at these restaurants and would allow us to go there and sign. None of us had any money except for carfare.

The Horton Company was very much a family. Lester was the father, and when she was there, Bella Lewitzky was the mother. By the time I came back after my stay in San Francisco, Bella had left. Bella, her husband, and Lester's lover, Bill Bowne, were politically very far left of center. As a matter of fact, when I first started taking classes with the company, Bella took me to her house and introduced me to her library of Communist literature. Over many dinners she urged me to become part of the war against capitalist oppression of the working class. It was the time of the McCarthy hearings and the rumor was that Bella wanted Lester to publicly denounce them. Lester didn't do so, and that, it is said, led to more conflict between them.

Artistic differences between Lester and Bella grew to be just as intense as their political ones. We began to hear that Bella regarded Lester's direction as too entertainment oriented. She wanted the company to focus on pure modern concert dance. At least one of the reasons Lester took the popular path was to help his dancers occasionally get paying gigs, dancing in movies and nightclubs, so they could pay rent and eat. A big explosion between two such headstrong people was inevitable, and when it came, Bella, her husband, and Lester's lover left. It was a difficult breakup. They had built this theater together over twenty-five years, and they had accomplished so much—creating scores and teaching so many gifted students. The artistic relationship between the two of them had been nearly spiritual in its intensity. To see them work together on ballets such as *Salome* and *Beloved* was an unforgettable experience for young artists such as myself. Suddenly it was all gone. After Bella left, Lester had his first heart attack, in July 1950. Lester's students—including me—always said that she broke his heart, and I still think it's true. They were so close—it would be as if Carmen and I suddenly decided we couldn't be bothered with each other. My heart would be broken.

With Bella gone, everyone wondered who was going to dance the role of Salome. "Carmen," Lester said very calmly. The reaction of some people was "Ha! Ha! Eighteen-year-old Carmen doing a hot role like Salome? Puh-*leeeze!* Bella is the only Salome in the world." For most of us at the studio—but not for me—Carmen was simply this little girl in the back of the studio doing intermediate and advanced classes. She was very shy and withdrawn. How could she possibly replace Bella?

But she did, and she hasn't looked back since. Carmen was an instant star. She had incredible talent and incredible charisma, and, at nineteen, she was the most beautiful woman in the world. Savage and sexy are the words I would use to describe her. Immediately upon assuming the Salome role, Lester made dance after dance tailored specifically for her, just as I did for Judy Jamison in my company. For the rest of his life, Carmen was the radiant star of the Lester Horton Dance Theater; Jimmy Truitte was the leading male dancer. It was quite revolutionary at the time to have a mixed company with two black people as lead dancers. But being on the West Coast helped. There are a lot of black people, Asians, and Mexicans in Los Angeles, so the idea of fusion was strong. Martha Graham managed a mixed company on the East Coast (in the late fifties she had Mary Hinkson and Clive Thompson), though not to the extent that Lester did. Lester was in the vanguard, and what he did was inevitable. He realized that you have to use the best dancers regardless of color.

My first performance with the company was an awful experience. I have always had these terrible feelings about myself, that I didn't belong and couldn't perform adequately. I didn't feel very much like a dancer and was convinced that my body just couldn't do it. I can understand now why Lester was interested in me as a dancer—what I brought to it is what a gymnast brings. In those days I had a very stretched back, very stretched legs, and, I guess you could say, the body of life. There were no mirrors in Lester's studio, so I never knew what I looked like as a dancer until I got to New York City, where all the studios had mirrors. Part of my struggle with feelings of inferiority was understandable. There were other people there who were simply better. Jimmy Truitte was a wonderful dancer; so were Don Martin and Jack Dobbs. They could do all the things Lester wanted them to do on the count of three. I couldn't do them till count nine. Then there was the problem of my feet. Lester spent a lot of time trying to make my stone feet more flexible.

The first time you performed for Lester he showed you how to put your makeup on. He applied it for you once, and then you were supposed to do it like that forevermore. He had what he considered a proven Asian theory about makeup: you put on a base, then powder it. After that, you do the lines on your face, apply more pancake, then all the structure. The result is very natural looking.

One day he said to me, "I want you to learn *The Batucada.* You're going to be in it." "Oh, no, not *The Batucada,*" I thought. It has rhythms that one has to stomp out in clogs. I spent hours in the back of the studio trying to learn this dance, but I never did get a successful hold on it; I never really understood it. Still, I did *The Batucada,* and I was awful. I didn't do anything right—not one single solitary thing. There were ten people in it, and I was in the back, so nobody knew how bad I was—except me. After it was over, I ran to the dressing room, ripped off my costume, removed my makeup, and left. And I didn't go back for a while.

Finally Lester called and asked, "What happened?" I was still upset. "I was awful," I said, "and I can't come back. I didn't do anything right. I was on the wrong beat. I wasn't hearing the music right." Lester said, "It wasn't as bad as you thought it was, Alvin, and you know perfectly well you have to come back." I had used that brief interlude to dance in a nightclub, but Lester was convinced that my immediate future was with him. This time I moved out near the Horton Theater so I wouldn't have to travel by bus for one and a half hours.

There was a lot going on in the theater. Lester rented the lot next door and broke out a wall to make more room for a children's program. The program wasn't just dance either—the children did sculpture, created paper figures, learned choreography, and wrote music. It was all about teaching and absorbing creativity, and it was a wonderful experience for the children.

Once I returned there, I felt the financial pinch and took a job at a hamburger stand about three blocks down from the Horton studio. Ralph and Laura, my bosses, I'll never forget, nor can I thank them enough. They fixed my hours so I could be with Lester and the studio and not miss valuable rehearsal time.

There was still no likelihood that we could make a living from dance. We were doing it because we loved it and because we loved Lester. We realized how full we felt; we were surrounded by music and dancing and joy. And Lester was just superb. We emulated him. He was a fantastic role model, even down to the way he dressed. He had American Indian shirts and big Navajo buckles. Sometimes he would dress up more formally in a gray suit with a pink shirt and green tie. It always amazed me that the state of Indiana had produced such a contemporary, cosmopolitan man of the world. When we were with him, we felt we were in many places at once, always surrounded by music, dancing, and joy. He was a wonderful man, and I am forever grateful that I crossed his path.

What I've been trying to do through all the years with my school and my company is to create that feeling of love, of caring, that we had with Lester. Lester's approach was to give you the feeling that you and he were creating together. He never made you feel: "I'm doing this." Instead it was: "We're doing this together." Lester would say, "We're going to buy some costumes, family." He knew every fabric in the world and was extremely knowledgeable about color, design, dyeing, and tailoring. He would touch, feel, even smell, the fabric. He taught us which fabrics worked in movement and which kind of skirt would create a flurry onstage. He loved fashioning gorgeous costumes from chiffon, velvet, and jersey when most other modern companies were dancing in woolen dresses. He also taught us to shop in notion stores for materials and other things that could be added to costumes—buttons, bows, flowers, and ruffles. We would help sew these on his creations. I am still guided by Lester's insistence that costumes must be made from extraordinary fabric, must be extraordinarily colorful, must be for the person who's wearing it, and must almost have a life of its own. When I finally became a choreographer, I took all of that with me, all of his ideas about sharing and about being a family. When I made my first ballet after he died, I did exactly what he did, and from that moment on I have always insisted on proper costumes and sets for my ballets.

Lester died suddenly. He drank a lot. After the initial heart attack, he wasn't supposed to eat certain things, and he wasn't supposed to touch alcohol. But with all the problems of running a school, he couldn't help himself. You could tell when he had been drinking because he would come in reeking of booze.

It was Lester's custom to create what we called a Bal Caribe, a Caribbean Ball. He used his knowledge of ethnic dance in 1951 to make a stylized suite of dances, *Tropic Trio*, that we could do in nightclubs and in films, as well as onstage, to earn money. In 1953 he created a very erotic suite of five dances called *Dedication to José Clemente Orozco*. One of the segments of that suite was "Cumbia." He came to me after he had completed "Cumbia" and said, "It's time for you to get started, Alvin, so I'm going to make this a dance for you and Carmen." I was scared to death because she was such a goddess to me. Here Carmen was his lead dancer, and I was this country bumpkin who was athletic and could wiggle a little. I was completely dazzled by Carmen's lyricism, emotion, passion, and beauty. How could I possibly dance with her?

But Lester insisted I was ready. I was trembling all the time, but audiences went absolutely wild over the two of us.

We didn't do *Orozco* in the Horton Theater; Lester rented Earl Carroll's, a big nightclub, to do a benefit for the school, and the audience dressed up and paid fifty dollars—an outrageous amount for the early fifties. Word of our success traveled, and we were asked to do *Orozco* in Ciro's, a nightclub that had featured a lot of big bands, including Dunham and Company and the Jack Cole dancers. Now, thrillingly, it featured the Horton dancers. After the performance that afternoon, when I returned home, I received a phone call that Lester had had a heart attack and died while I was onstage at Ciro's with Carmen. I remember sitting on the bus, going out to the studio after hearing what had happened. Everybody was just sitting, quietly mourning his loss. It was a very bad time for all of us. It was evident that at forty-seven, the drinking had caught up with him. And that was when forty-seven became my mortal number. I was twenty-two and was absolutely convinced that I would die before I reached forty-seven, the age when Lester left us.

With the great man gone, the whole place took on a different cast. It was as though someone had turned on a blue light. I was frozen with anxiety. How would we go on? What would happen without him? Lester had been everything creative, and we knew next to nothing about choreography. Lester was one of those people who did choreography all by himself, and as we were scheduled to open our season at a theater called the Wiltshire, we needed a new choreographer fast. Frank Eng, our general manager, got us all together and said that we had to open the season with a new ballet. "Next week we will meet again," he said. "I want all of you to come back with ideas about making a ballet."

Even back then I always had several notebooks full of nota-tions—little poems, scrawled ideas about this or that, costume drawings. During that week I came up with several ideas, one being a tribute to Lester that related him to St. Francis of Assisi. It was called *According to St. Francis*. Another was a dance called *Mourning Morning*, which I couldn't get quite right for Carmen. I had to make dances for Lester's lead dancers, Jimmy Truitte, Carmen, Joyce Trisler—the three people I loved. I built the St. Francis of Assisi piece on Jimmy.

I arrived for the follow-up meeting with four ideas in all. Eng wasn't eager to follow in Lester's footsteps, so for lack of anyone else, I became the appointed choreographer.

I'll never forget the night before our first rehearsal. I stayed at the studio, too excited to go home, too excited to sleep; I sprawled out on benches in the studio trying to get my ideas together. My score was written by a black woman composer, Gertrude Rivers Robinson, who had worked with Lester on his last ballet. My decor and costumes were designed by Larry War-ren, one of the dancers. My main source of worry was how I would start the ballet. How could I possibly choreograph Jimmy?

But once rehearsals started, I drove Jimmy completely out of my mind and concentrated all my thoughts on making the ballet work. *St. Francis* ran an hour when I completed it, and Frank said, "Don't you think this is a little long?" I said, "What do you mean?" I was furious that he questioned its length, but I finally got it down to about fifty minutes. Poor Jimmy, he must have lost about twenty-five pounds. He was onstage the whole time and was forced to dance in weird positions that put tremendous stress on his body. "Alvin," he kept asking me, "don't you think I should go offstage once in a while?" "No," I kept telling him, "you're the leading man, you have to be on."

Frank always said that I wanted to be Lester Horton. Because I had been so close to Lester and was in awe of him, it must have showed in my work and attitude. When I started doing choreography, I was Lester all over again—Lester reincarnated. I told everybody, "Let's repaint the floors." "Let's redye these things." "Let's make all your costumes." "Let's go find the fabric for you." I played music when people were working. I did Lester completely.

The reactions to my first two ballets are faint in my memory. They were really kitchen-sink ballets in that they contained everything I'd ever dreamed of—fifty minutes, in the case of *St. Francis,* with nothing left out that I could possibly imagine. In *Mourning Morning,* my second ballet, I took everything Tennessee Williams had ever written and put it onstage. And I did this with a cast of three people. It was so confusing that I'm sure nobody knew what was going on onstage.

Probably the most memorable thing about these two ballets is that my mother saw them. When I first started going to the Horton School, I don't think she knew exactly what I was doing, but she did know that I was completely engrossed in my work. By that time I had had a lot of passions in my life; my mother had lived with me through my passions for literature, for butterflies, for writing the Great American Novel, and for turning out reams of poetry, so she thought I was just off on one more passion. By the time she and my stepfather finally came out to see what I was doing, Lester had died and I had created new choreography for the studio. They didn't quite understand what to make of it, but even so, they thought it was beautiful.

The two ballets were next performed at Jacob's Pillow in Massachusetts, in 1954. The company had been there two years before, in 1952, when Lester was still alive. Ted Shawn, who ran Jacob's Pillow, had fallen in love with the company and with Lester, so he invited us to come back. Since we had to have new ballets, it was decided to take my two. The *St. Francis* ballet now had some big trees in it made out of plaster, and after looking at a Martha Graham work I decided that I had to have these trees draped with fabric. We transported these trees across the country to Jacob's Pillow.

Twelve, maybe fourteen, of us made the trip. We had two cars and a station wagon with all the scenery in it. On the way to Jacob's Pillow, we stopped in New York City for a couple of days. Monty King, one of the interesting people who hung around the Horton Company, was always trying to get engagements for us so we could make some money. He had arranged an audition for those of us in the Latin dance "Cumbia" for producers, for television, and for anyone else who might be interested. Following the audition set up by Monty, there was an audition in the same space for *House of Flowers*, a Broadway-bound musical. So its producers also saw us.

Carmen and I danced lead in "Cumbia." Janet Collins came up to us immediately after we finished and told us that one of the producers of *House of Flowers* thought we could be in his show. We said, "Oh, no! We don't want to do Broadway. We're concert dancers," and went on to Jacob's Pillow.

It turned out that Ted Shawn, the great father of American modern dance, hated my ballets, just hated them. He wrote a letter to Frank saying, "How dare you let this young man bring these ballets, these unfinished ballets with no form and no structure, to Jacob's Pillow, the haven of modern dance?" He was very angry and disappointed.

Back in California after the Jacob's Pillow disaster, Carmen and I received a telephone call at Horton's house, where some of us had been living since his death. We were invited to join the cast of *House of Flowers*. These were the producers we had stunned, who had seen us dance in New York City the previous summer at the Alvin Theatre, and apparently they thought we would make important contributions to their show.

It's no exaggeration to say their call caused an uproar in the Horton organization. Here I was, the new choreographer trying to fill Lester Horton's shoes and a kind of spiritual leader of the Horton Company, and here was Carmen, Lester's wonderful, beautiful, extraordinarily talented lead dancer. How could we even consider going east to appear in a commercial Broadway musical? Frank Eng was not very happy at the thought. He was convinced we would be completely corrupted and would lose the essence of what Lester had taught us about modern dance. I, on the other hand, wanted very much to study with the East Coast moderns—people like Martha Graham, Hanya Holm, Charles Weidman, and anybody else back east who could show me new directions, as Lester had done. All that I knew about dance and choreography at that point in my career I had learned from Lester. They had been wonderful, wonderful lessons, but I was curious about what else was out there. So I saw joining *House of Flowers,* and being a lead dancer, as an opportunity to expand my horizons and then later bring it all back to California.

As for Carmen, she and I both felt it was time for her to move on. She was already a star. When Bella left, Carmen had risen fast; critics and the public adored her. Another factor in our thinking was that we all felt a little lost without Lester. He had been our guiding light; he had meant everything to us. Without him, we didn't know quite where we were going artistically. So, after three or four days of deliberation Carmen and I decided to go east and join *House of Flowers.* I promised on a stack of Bibles that we would come back to the Horton organization the minute the show was over. Promise or not, I never did make it back to California.

In retrospect, I now realize that the pressing need to keep things functioning after Lester's sudden death had allowed us practically no time to deal with our shock and grief over his death. Jimmy Truitte, Don Martin, Frank Eng, and the others kept the company going for another four years before it dissolved for good in 1958. Members of the Horton artistic family went on to make marvelous contributions to dance and other professions. Joyce Trisler, who left for New York before Carmen and I, danced with my company for years and founded her own company before her early death in 1979. Jimmy eventually went to New York on a Whitney fellowship and is still a master teacher of the Horton technique. Don Martin has danced all over the world. Marge (Berman) Perces teaches with the Alvin Ailey American Dance Theater's school. And Yvonne de Lavallade became a much sought after dancer.

Lester was a great artist, a great teacher, and a great, great human being, and he has not received his due for his major contributions to modern dance, especially for having the vision and the courage to transcend the racism that plagued and too often still plagues decision making in the dance world. One of the few times he received credit was in a July 2, 1961, issue of the *New York Times*. I quote writer Arthur Todd in full:

"Another major teacher-choreographer, the late Lester Horton of California, was responsible for bringing four of today's major dancers to fruition.

"The first is Janet Collins, who arrived in New York in 1949 and moved like a dream personified. She danced in Cole Porter's *Out of This World* and in the Metropolitan Opera's production of *Aida*.

"Carmen de Lavallade, one of the most beautiful dancers in America, both physically and technically, has appeared on television with the New York City Opera and a number of modern dance companies and is a guest dancer with Alvin Ailey.

"James Truitte, another alumnus of the Horton School, has made notable appearances in the East and is, perhaps, the finest teacher of the Horton Method, a technique that seems to be of considerable value in the contemporary field.

"Alvin Ailey, the fourth Horton disciple, made his impact on Broadway as the lead dancer in two musicals, *House of Flowers* and *Jamaica*. Two concerts at the 92nd Street Y.M. and Y.W.-H.A. and another at the Clark Center of the Young Women's Christian Association (where he now teaches) have established him as the greatest male dancer in his field today and as a choreographer of enormous talent."

To provide further insight into Lester as an artist and a human being, Carmen and Marge Perces, at my request, made the following observations:

Carmen said:

"Lester was a generous and brilliant artist and humanitarian who knew how to connect with people and how to build them up as human beings as well as dancers. He knew how to find the hidden parts of his dancers and then bring them forward. Lester taught us every aspect of dance and of being a part of the dance world. This included teaching us not only dance technique but other crucial things, such as stage etiquette and how to differentiate between healthy competition and the more destructive kind. His reasoning was that each of us is unique and has had unique things to offer as dancers. Thus there is no reason for jealousy. Lester's choreography is logical in that its movements are those that one normally does in such circumstances. He taught not only movement but also the underneath, the soul of what we were doing and why we were doing it. He was very much interested in performance, what comes out of my body. Lester also taught us to be open to dance forms from a variety of sources, just as he was. It was this same openness that spurred Lester to transcend the racial climate of his time and create a truly multiethnic company. Lester, the man, the artist, and the teacher, was a master in each area."

And Marjorie (Berman) Perces said: "Lester had a special talent for investigating movement. He was very concerned with each dancer's body, so his technique focused on developing weaker parts of the body—feet, back, abdominal muscles. He created new motions with quite simple lines that are eminently achievable by dancers. His technique also focused on motion designed to extend joint mobility and on constant explorations of methods for descending to and ascending from the floor into horizontal positions. Thus it has the potential to evoke a rich variety of expressive motions. Lester was able to teach and inspire dancers to excellence not only because he was talented; he was also warm, open, giving, expressive, and humorous."

SIX

My Fling in the Theater

*I*t was a dark, very windy evening when Carmen and I boarded a four-motor airplane and were shipped off to Philadelphia. We were met at the airport by the company manager. My next memory is of sitting in the audience in the Erlanger Theater, where *House of Flowers* was in rehearsals, and seeing the incredible show we would soon be a part of. Some of the most dazzling black talent of that time was there. Diahann Carroll, at nineteen, was making her Broadway debut. She was very shy, very much into herself, not at all the glamour girl she would become. There was Rawn Spearman, a fantastic tenor; Juanita Hall, Pearl Bailey, Geoffrey Holder. Carmen and I sat there wide-eyed, studying all that fantastic talent we were about to join.

Most of the choreography was by George Balanchine. There was startling scenery by Oliver Messel and wonderful music and lyrics by Yip Harburg and Harold Arlen, who loved Diahann Carroll. Arlen spent much of his time gently holding her hands when she sang "I Never Has Seen Snow," trying to get the notes right.

Herbert Ross had taken over the choreography from Mr. Balanchine. Carmen and I had worked with him in *Carmen Jones* with Dorothy Dandridge, Harry Belafonte, Otto Preminger, and Pearl Bailey. He had gotten to know us, and along with producer Arnold Saint-Subber, had decided that we had to be in the show. So there we were in Philadelphia onstage at the Erlanger Theater, with me trembling as I watched all the gifted people who were also going to be in the show—so much outrageous talent! There were Pearl Reynolds, Mary Montoya, Arthur Mitchell, Lou Comacho, Louis Johnson; there were all those squirming, vibrant, energetic, well-trained New York dancers waiting to see what Carmen and I were going to do. We were importees—two young people who had been brought in from way across the country and presented to them as lead dancers.

Aware of the tension, Herb Ross spared us the pain of being choreographed in front of the company. Instead, he called us early the next morning and began working with us on a wonderful duet. One scene had Carmen and me wrapped around each other while crawling on the floor. (It would later bring the house down.) He also choreographed a dance for me called *Slide, Boy, Slide,* and danced to a song sung by Juanita Hall in her role as Madame Tango, it was exactly that. I spent much of the time sliding on my knees, my back, my shoulders, my head, and whatever part of my body Ross could invent a slide for. I loved every minute of it.

On the day we joined the company, Carmen and I went backstage and saw this tall gentleman in the show named Geoffrey Holder. When his eyes lit on Miss de Lavallade, they immediately widened with excitement and interest. After that, the pursuit was on. Geoffrey never gave Carmen a minute's peace. Wherever Carmen was, Geoffrey would be there beside her. And, much to my dismay, the chase finally ended in their marriage. I had been in love with Carmen de Lavallade forever, it seemed, and I didn't want anybody to marry her, though I was not prepared to marry her myself. Carmen and I had known each other since high school. She had taken me to Lester Horton. I knew her aunt and her father. Somehow, the idea that Carmen would not be attached to me but married to this oversized man was something it took me a long time to adjust to.

The Philadelphia run of *House of Flowers* was a success, particularly after the conflict between Pearl Bailey, the star of the show, and the director, Peter Brook, was resolved. Apparently, before Carmen and I came to the show, Brook had made a racist remark that Bailey found very offensive. She also apparently had problems with his direction and the way he gave her notes. It reached a point where Bailey would faint anytime Peter Brook appeared in the theater. Management finally decided that he should be dismissed. One day, when we came to rehearsal, he was no longer the director; Truman Capote, the show's writer, had replaced him. Capote had decided that the only way to get juice out of his lines was to do the coaching himself. So this tiny man sat in a huge shawl in the chill of the theater, giving corrections to everybody in his tiny voice. His reign as director lasted only a couple of days. Herbert Ross then took over.

I never got to know Capote well. When Carmen and I first joined the cast, he was usually around to do constant rewrites. He impressed me as being a shy person who dressed rather extravagantly in a series of huge shawls, fashionable glasses, and other precious accoutrement. When we would go to New York City, Truman constantly urged me to take over an old Rolls-Royce limousine he owned. "Listen, Alvin," he would say in that tiny voice, "I want you to have the Rolls because I'm really tired of it. Can't you do wonderful things with this limousine?" I never knew if he was jesting or serious, but I didn't accept his offer. After we opened on Broadway, I didn't see much of him. My lasting impression is that he was a terribly gentle, terribly sensitive, and also terribly sad man.

We went from Philadelphia to the Alvin Theatre on Broadway, which I thought was very appropriate—Alvin at the Alvin. *House of Flowers* lasted five months on Broadway, receiving mixed reviews from the critics. For me it was a glowing, vibrant show, and everybody loved its visual power. The colors and costumes were extraordinary; the music was wonderful. I had never seen so much black talent crammed into one show. There's an old saying that there are so many of us around who are talented and so few shows for all of us to appear in.

At that time, I was a lively, athletic, not terribly well trained dancer, with, at twenty-four, a lot of physical charisma. I thought the height of choreographic drama was to jump as high as you could and land on your knees. I also knew my limitations and was willing to learn. I fell in love with Louis Johnson, Pearl Reynolds, and Arthur Mitchell and studied hard under them. It was during this period that I met Karel Shook, who helped to found the Dance Theater of Harlem and who had a little postage stamp of a dance studio on Eighth Avenue between Forty-fourth and Forty-fifth Streets. His classes were filled with dancers like Mary Hinkson, Carmen, Geoffrey, Arthur, Matt Turney, and other members of the black dance world who were serious about performing. He was a philosopher, a father, and a rough guy who was a very important influence on me and many other dancers in the mid-fifties.

Karel Shook attracted black dancers because nobody else wanted us to study with them. He welcomed us. We all owed him money, but he insisted that we still come to class. One day, when Carmen, Geoffrey, Arthur, Matt Turney, Mary Hinkson, Ted Crumb, Sylvester Campbell, and I were working out at the bar in his studio, he told us, "You are all talented people, and you gotta be in these classes."

Arthur Mitchell, at the time, lived with Shook on Thirty-fourth Street and First Avenue. He was not yet in the New York City Ballet. I used to go to their place, and they would feed me.

Arthur wanted to be a classical dancer, but his ankles, back then, were not strong and flexible enough for ballet. So he did a thousand battements tendus every night to stretch the feet and make his ankles more supple.

Shook used to cook and also supervise Arthur's rehearsals. I would sit and watch or sometimes read. Shook often said to me: "You say you want to be a choreographer, but you don't read history. You don't go to museums. Alvin, you're full of shit. You're not going to be a choreographer. You don't even know anything about music. Do you know Beethoven's Ninth Symphony?" He was a real mentor—not a Lester Horton, but tough. I spent a lot of time with Arthur and Karel Shook. They were very helpful to me.

After *House of Flowers*, there was a long period of unemployment, and I wondered if I was going to be able to keep myself together in New York City. Finally, feeling the money pinch, I moved downtown, just east of Greenwich Village, the home of poets, writers, and choreographers—right in the heart, I thought back then, of New York's creative center. My room was on Ninth Street, between Third and Fourth Avenues. The building is still there. I lived on unemployment benefits and was hungry most of the time. I often went to a restaurant across the street and put a lot of water in the soup. There were many interesting bars in the Village, and I partied a lot; I also searched out all the movie theaters that showed foreign films. For a year I did little serious work.

I felt good about myself after *House of Flowers*. For the first time in my life people knew who Alvin Ailey was. It was a strange and exciting feeling to be recognized by people I didn't know, but my little bit of fame wasn't helping me get a job. During that period I studied occasionally with Hanya Holm. I hated that. In fact, I was going through a period of intense hostility toward the whole New York modern dance scene. I didn't like José Limón. I didn't like Merce Cunningham. I didn't like anybody. The trouble was they just were not Lester Horton. Lester had set the standards I aspired to, and, next to him, they were not creative; they were too much like ballet; they didn't teach any technique other than their own. After all, I knew what had to be done. I had all these creative vibes bubbling inside. I taught some classes in which I tried to interpret the Horton technique with a style of my own, but I felt I was spinning wheels. Even with my newfound notoriety I wasn't happy. I thought seriously about getting out of New York and returning to California.

Two years after moving to Greenwich Village, I finally did crawl out. I decided that the Village was not the place for serious creative work, in spite of all the painters and writers who lived there. It was a very distracting place to me, so I moved to the Upper West Side. Desperately in need of a job, I went to my friend the choreographer Donnie McKayle and explained my position. Here I was, a young dancer from California, with a good show behind me—but definitely behind me—and my unemployment benefits had run out. He said, "Okay, I'm going to give you a job in *Show Boat.*" Just like that! So Donnie hired me for a summer production of *Show Boat,* which I remember as much for the windy weather at Jones Beach, where we were performing, as anything else. We wore feathery costumes in an African scene in which I was one of sixteen guys who came out bearing spears. It was a wonderful experience but not a high point for me, since I was relegated to the back. On the bus ride to Jones Beach I met some of the other dancers appearing in *Show Boat,* including Ernie Parham, with whom I eventually did my first concert.

Later that year, 1956, I was asked to be in a show with Harry Belafonte called *Sing, Man, Sing,* which was scheduled to tour the country. Harry knew me from California, back before the calypso rage vaulted him into the limelight. He was out on the West Coast making the movie *Carmen Jones* with Dorothy Dandridge. In his spare time Harry started coming around and watching the Horton School rehearsals. Julie Robinson, whom Harry would later marry, attended the Horton School, but it became clear that he was mad about Carmen de Lavallade. She was the one who drew him back for rehearsals day after day. He took Carmen home a couple of times. We all believed—and I still believe—that if Carmen had said yes, she would have become Mrs. Belafonte.

Harry asked me to choreograph *Sing, Man, Sing*. Very few people in New York City were aware that I was a choreographer, but he had seen my first ballets at the Horton Theater and had been impressed. When he approached me about choreographing his musical, I was terrified. I said, "No, I really don't want to do it." Then he said, "Well, anyway, you should dance in it, Alvin." He got Walter Nicks, an experienced choreographer, to do the choreography and hired Mary Hinkson as the leading female dancer. I played the role of Harry's alter ego; Mary played the leading singing lady, Margaret Time. We set out across the country touring, and Mary Hinkson and I had some major problems. She was constantly lecturing me about my dancing; she was convinced that my deficiencies, as she saw them, were the result of my never taking classes. In partnering I would grasp her arm when I was supposed to hold her hand. The conductor played the music in ways that were strange to me, and sometimes I would do unpredictable things onstage. "You never do the same thing twice," Mary kept complaining. She wanted Harry to fire me and bring in Arthur Mitchell to dance my part. Harry refused.

We had a love-hate relationship, Harry and I. I was still in Levi's in those days, and he would always criticize the way I dressed. I looked a mess—at least, that's what I thought until one day outside the theater I saw a huge picture of me and Harry and the other members of the cast. "Who is that guy?" I wondered. I was staring at a long, tall, muscular character in a loincloth, and with his high cheekbones he looked like my mother. It was the first time I realized I was not a bad-looking man.

There was antagonism between Harry and me because I didn't consider him a true folksinger. As I've mentioned, it was the time of the calypso, and the world had bestowed on Harry the title of the world's greatest folksinger. Now I had spent many hours in the Los Angeles Public Library listening to all the folk music in the world. I would tell Harry, "You are not a folksinger. You are not Blind Lemon Jefferson. What you're singing is commercialized pop." He would get very angry when I talked to him like that.

Sing, Man, Sing taught me a lot about touring. Watching the show being put together, watching how things were staged, was a wonderful lesson for me. It also put some money in my pocket. When I came back from tour I started doing concerts with other people, including Sophie Maslow, who is a part of modern dance history. Anna Sokolow asked me to do a part that Donnie McKayle had just performed in her ballet.

Later on, after pursuing my studies, mainly with Karel Shook in classical dance, Christyne Lawson and I decided to become a dance team. She lived down the street from me in Los Angeles and was an exceptional artist in dance. I would do all the choreography, and we were going to startle the world with our greatness. There hadn't been a black dance team since Talley Beatty and Janet Collins, and our time, we felt, had arrived. We put together some Jack Cole–like routines before coming to New York. I had worked with Cole in California on a film called *Lydia Bailey*. I was impressed by his style, by the way he danced, by his manner, by the masculinity of his projection, by his fierceness, by his animal-like qualities. I was happy to be imitating a man whose choreography I so greatly admired.

Christyne and I auditioned for a show Cole was choreo-graphing called *Jamaica,* and we were taken on as lead dancers. *Jamaica* starred Lena Horne and Ricardo Montalban and was a marvelous experience, mainly because of Jack Cole. To me, he was an artistic genius, a powerhouse dancer, and a neurotic kind of choreographer (he had to make everybody angry with him before he could choreograph), with a legend from here to eter-nity tied to him.

He gave the dancers, who included Billy Wilson, Pearl Rey-nolds, Audrey Mason, and Barbara Wright, complex, complex steps that they were supposed to pick up immediately. Nobody could do so, with the possible exception of Clive Thompson. Because I had a hard time figuring out Cole's style, he was al-ways on me. "Alvin, you're dancing like you're on skis." He complained that I was always doing poses from the classics. "Don't pose! Don't pose! *Move.* Dancing is *movement,*" he would scream at me. While my feet were bleeding and my knees aching, he would scream at me, showing me how to do his steps correctly, with flair, with great verve, with great style. I could never do anything right for Jack Cole; I don't think I ever did one thing perfectly right.

After rehearsals some of us would go to a bar down the street, drink martinis, and stagger home. No matter how much Cole got on me, *Jamaica* was a wonderful experience. I loved every minute of it. I still carry with me an image of Jack Cole as this ferocious man, this ferocious animal. The image influenced my dancing and the style I projected up to the moment I stopped dancing in 1965.

We went out of town with *Jamaica* to the Shubert Theater in Boston. I saw the Shubert Theater the other day when my com-pany was performing across the street in this enormous space called the Wang Center. The Wang Center has a four-thousand-seat auditorium. Beside it, the Shubert now looks like a dollhouse, but when we went there with *Jamaica*, I remember marveling at how enormous it was.

Lena Horne was adorable, absolutely marvelous. She was a great friend of the dancers and would often come to rehearsals early just to watch what the dancers were doing. Many times when she came, she had just been to Mr. John's or some furrier and would be decked out in leopard or mink. She would stand quietly on the side, sort of waiting to see if anybody recognized that she had on something new. She was not happy until somebody came by and asked, "What's this?" "It's nothing. Just a little leopard hat from Mr. John's," she would say. I loved it. She used to call me "Earth Man." She was always very encouraging. "I like the way you move, Earth Man," she would say to me.

There was a constant rivalry and a real sense of friction between Lena Horne and Josephine Premice. They very seldom spoke and managed not to be on the same part of the stage at the same time. We in the company took sides; there was a Josephine group and a Lena group. We who were anti-Premice made up all sorts of wonderfully bitchy things about what she was wearing that day. "Did you see that silver motorcycle jacket Josephine is wearing?" we would say. "Lena would *never* wear a silver motorcycle jacket. I bet it's from S. Klein's." Lena would then come in wearing some exquisite piece from Yves St. Laurent. "Now *that's* the way to dress," we would say. It was said that Lena was happy I was in her camp; it helped to balance things, because Josephine stopped the show every night with a song called "Leave the Atom Alone."

The show did very well, even though the reviews were only moderately good. *Jamaica* proved to be my last musical. In the middle of August 1961, Michael Shurtleff, a playwright who worked for producer David Merrick, approached me. He said, "I've written this play, *Call Me by My Rightful Name*. We want you to read for it." I said, "Why me? I've never acted or even studied acting." He said, "Yeah, but we think you're right for the part." Not knowing what to expect, I met the director and read for the part of a young black student who lives on campus with a white roommate. The roommates fight over a white girl. Shurtleff was a Method person. He said, "You don't have any training, Ailey, but I have the feeling that you can do this." I later learned that after seeing *Jamaica* Shurtleff had written the play with me in mind. My white roommate was played by a young actor named Robert Duvall, who was born on the same day of the same year as I was. The white girl was played by Joan Hackett.

We began rehearsals at the Clark Center in the Fifty-first Street YWCA and later moved downtown to One Sheridan Square. The play opens with my character staggering up the stairs drunk, about to have a confrontation with his roommate. I thought that as a Method actor I should get a little drunk for the first rehearsal and see what happened. I went to a bar around the corner, had a couple of martinis, came back to rehearsal, and staggered all over the place. Luckily for me, they thought it was funny and didn't fire me.

The show ran four months. It was a marvelous experience, and I learned a lot about acting. My notices, however, were terrible. The *Village Voice* critic said I just didn't know what I was doing, and he was probably right. I don't think it helped much, my appearing with two such superb actors as Hackett and Duvall. They were fabulous. But I learned from them and got more in touch with the acting community.

Duvall's roommate at the time was Dustin Hoffman. He was often around the theater. Both were madly in love with one of my dancers, Minnie Marshall, a dancer in my first concert in 1958. They thought she was the most beautiful woman they had ever seen. They used to come to our dance rehearsals, follow

Minnie around, and give her flowers and notes. When *Call Me by My Rightful Name* closed, I went back to the dance world.

Next came a William Saroyan play called *Talking to You.* This time I played the part of a boxer, Blackstone Boulevard, who befriends a child. The boxer's a little bit crazy and ends up shooting people. It was probably my most rewarding play. I got great notices, including a rave from Harold Clurman, Stella Adler's husband (by that time I had started studying with her). I found acting very difficult—really, really tough—and I got more stimulated by acting classes as a choreographer than as an actor. The memory exercises were especially useful because they have a lot to do with where my choreography was coming from. But I didn't see any great future for me as an actor; there was nowhere I could see myself going.

My next role was in *Ding Dong Bell,* a play done in summer stock with Albert Decker. I played a radical preacher in the civil rights movement. I was scared to death, but it went well and I held my own.

My last play was *Tiger, Tiger, Burning Bright.* The producers had been searching around for a long time for someone to play the part I ended up with. They had talked about casting Harry Belafonte, Sidney Poitier, and James Earl Jones—all fantastic actors. When I was handed the script, I said, "Uh! Uh! This is the doing of Joshua Logan." In 1959 I had done an actor's benefit with my little group. I had choreographed a suite of blues in which there is a men's dance called *Mean Ol' Frisco,* during the course of which the men talk, sing, and dance. Josh Logan came backstage after the show and said, "Don't you think you'd rather be an actor than a dancer?" I said, "I'm a choreographer, a dancer." Yet, two years later, we were sitting in Josh Logan's office and he was saying, "This is the man to do this part."

I was an old hand at reading for plays by then; this was my fourth one. So I got myself together and read for the part. It was an interesting play based on a novel by Peter Fiebleman. Set in New Orleans, it told the story of a dysfunctional family with a son, Tiger, about my age. He was a hustler and dope addict.

About a week after my reading, Josh Logan called my agent and said he wanted to take us both to dinner. At a fancy East Side restaurant, Logan offered me the part. "Who else is going to be in it?" I asked. "Oh, Diana Sands will be the girl next door," Logan said. "Cicely Tyson will be your sister. Al Freeman Jr. will be your little brother. Claudia McNeil will be your mother." It went on and on, star after star. Ellen Holly was in it. Roscoe Lee Browne was the minister. Robert McBeth was the soldier who had a walk-on. Billy Dee Williams was my understudy. (He never got on, by the way.) And I was the center of the play; my character was onstage all the time.

On the first day of rehearsals in the Booth Theatre, they discovered they couldn't hear me from the stage to the third row. So every day I was sent off to a speech teacher to learn how to be heard beyond the third row. I was doing Shakespeare at seven o'clock every morning to improve my projection.

Claudia McNeil, whose name was over the title, was the star of the show. We already knew about her reputation for being very temperamental. Diana Sands had warned us to be very careful with her because she had slapped Diana when they were in *Raisin in the Sun*. I was open and adoring around her. I thought, Look at this woman. She's playing this mother; why couldn't she play Electra? I was astounded by her power, and I was equally astounded by other people in the cast who knew exactly what they were doing. I had two scenes with each of them and felt unsure of myself and intimidated by their professionalism. I began drinking wine and then trying to hide my breath from the others. I knew drinking before a performance was a terrible thing to do, but the insecurity was hard to deal with.

Things went reasonably well for about three weeks. Then one day when we were about to leave rehearsals, Claudia said, "Just a minute. I want to have a meeting. All you young people sit down. Sit down!" So we all sat down on benches facing her. "I want to tell you *one* thing," she said. "That is that *I am a star."* Our mouths flew open. She said, "I am the star of this show. It is *my* name that raised the money for this show. It is *I* who have been suffering in the theater all these years with Langston Hughes plays and making a place for us all. *I* am the star of this show, and don't you *ever* forget it." Then she threw her huge mink around her shoulders and swept out the door, leaving us dumbfounded.

After that the war was on. There was antagonism between Claudia and all the rest of us. The writer Gay Talese documented another incident from *Tiger, Tiger* in *Esquire* some time ago. I was Claudia's son in the play and had to sit at her knee in one scene listening to her give a long speech. I was hovering there when she suddenly said, "Who is that? Somebody is walking around in a white coat in the back of the theater breaking my concentration." It was Joshua Logan. He yelled up to her, "Go ahead, Claudia. It's just me and the author. We're trying to fix some of the lines for you." "I don't want any of my lines fixed," she said. "Just be still while I'm trying to remember what I'm supposed to say. Don't be buzzing around in the back." She began her speech again, and he continued buzzing around. She stopped once more, this time pushing me to the floor. "Listen," she shouted, "I told you to stop moving around in that white coat. It's distracting me." Joshua Logan said, "Claudia, I'm getting tired of you, too. You're walking around antagonizing everybody, acting like a queen." She glared at him and said, "Honey, *you're* the queen. If there's any queen around here, it's *you*. You need to stop buzzing around. This play has to open up in three weeks, and you aren't doing a goddamn thing." It went on between them for about twenty minutes. We all snuck quietly away.

Claudia was also a master—or a mistress—at upstaging other actors. There was a moment in the play when I said something to her that angered her and she was supposed to slap my face. It was opening night, and I was sitting across the kitchen table from her; when the moment came for the slap, she jumped her lines and knocked me halfway across the stage. I said, "Oh, *no!*" I was lying there delivering whatever lines I could give, and she went merrily along with her speeches.

Many scenes were played in the kitchen, and Claudia had a way of dropping dishes on my lines. She would be washing dishes, and I would say so-and-so, and the next thing the playgoer heard, right through my lines, was a dish crashing to the floor. Or the screen door would slam shut on my lines. She was a genius at the art of the upstage.

I loved Diana Sands, but she also had a habit of upstaging me. She was the girl next door who was leaving home to head north. In one scene, Joshua Logan had put me about halfway up the stage looking out to the audience while she gave a speech. Diana started in front of me with her back halfway to the audience. By the time she finished the speech, she was all the way upstage and I was sitting with my back to the audience. Every night she managed to maneuver me into limbo. "Don't let Diana do that to you. You're letting them all upstage you," Joshua Logan said. But I didn't know how to stop them.

After my experiences with these wonderful, sensitive, extremely talented theater people, I decided that acting was not for me. Acting was a serious, serious business that demanded devotion and endless study. It had come down to a choice between giving myself to acting or giving myself to dance. I was so intense about dance that I felt I was being untrue to myself by going out onstage as an actor without feeling the same intensity.

When I finally had to choose, my choice was dance, especially choreography.

Still, I learned a lot by osmosis from those theater folks. And from watching the level of production from off-Broadway to summer stock to a big Broadway musical like *Jamaica,* I learned more and more about how things are put together, about the philosophy of musicals, about dealing with temperament.

Not that I don't think I could have become a fine actor. I had an early encounter in California with James Edwards. We read scripts together before I knew anything about acting, and it all kind of came naturally. I was a natural Method person, but the commitment was lacking.

The only theater I did after *Tiger, Tiger, Burning Bright* was Langston Hughes's *Jericho Jim Crow.* I did that in 1963 only because of a direct request from Langston. He was very fond of Carmen and me. He had seen us dance a duet in *Roots of the Blues,* which I had choreographed for the two of us. After a performance at City College's Lewisohn Stadium, he invited us and a drummer named Shep Sheppard to dinner. Hughes and I became good friends and often used to meet and talk, usually about music and dance—he was very fond of and knowledgeable about both. I once considered creating a ballet based on his poem "Ask Your Mama." In fact, I still have five poems he gave me for possible choreographic consideration. So when Langston asked me to help out with his show, I readily agreed. I was credited as codirector with William Hairston.

My first credit as a choreographer for a theater production came in 1960, when I choreographed *Darkness of the Moon* for Vinette Carroll at the Harlem YMCA. Its marvelous cast included Roscoe Lee Browne, James Early Jones, Minnie Marshall, Shaunielle Perry, Isabel Sanford, Harold Scott, Clebert Ford, Clarence Williams III, Thelma Hill, Loretta Abbott, and Herman Howell. Ellis Haizlip was production manager.

Alvin *(second dancer from left)* in *Blues Suite* during the highly acclaimed tour of Southeast Asia in 1962. It was his first trip abroad. *(Courtesy of Dick Campbell)*

Alvin *(on ladder)* in *Blues Suite* during the 1962 tour of Southeast Asia. *(Courtesy of Dick Campbell)*

Alvin *(holding flowers)* on the 1962 tour of Southeast Asia.
(Courtesy of Dick Campbell)

Alvin *(third from left)*, Thelma Hill *(on his right)*, Carmen de Lavallade, and Brother John Sellers take curtain calls after a concert during the Southeast Asia tour. *(Courtesy of Dick Campbell)*

Alvin responds to questions on the Southeast Asia tour.
(Courtesy of Dick Campbell)

The opening segment of *Revelations* during the tour of Southeast Asia.
Many dance historians consider this the most memorable opening sequence
in all of modern dance. *(Courtesy of Dick Campbell)*

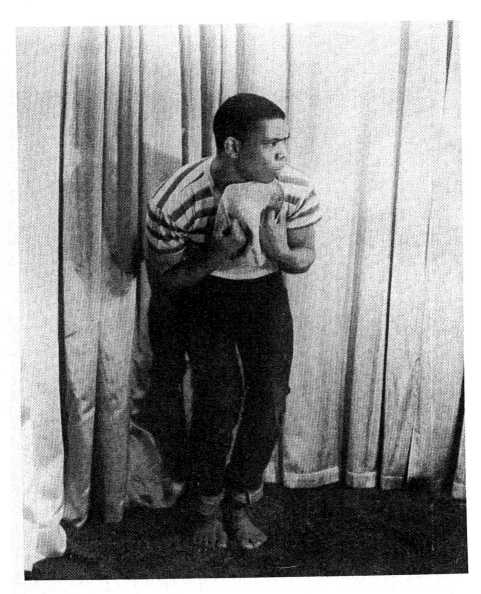

Alvin, in 1957, as a featured dancer in the Broadway musical *Jamaica*, which starred Lena Horne and Ricardo Montalban. *(Photo by Carl Van Vechten. Courtesy of Schomburg Center for Research in Black Culture)*

Alvin, with Lucinda Ransom *(holding umbrella)* and Loretta Abbott in
Revelations, which over the past thirty-five years has probably been seen
by more people than any other ballet created in the twentieth century.
(Courtesy of Schomburg Center for Research in Black Culture)

Joyce Trisler, Alvin's longtime friend, whose death in 1979 triggered a year of crisis for him. *(Courtesy of Schomburg Center for Research in Black Culture)*

Alvin and members of his company, with *Essence* editor in chief Susan Taylor directly behind Alvin. *(Courtesy of Schomburg Center for Research in Black Culture)*

SEVEN

The Early Years of the Alvin Ailey American Dance Theater

In 1958, there were many terrific black dancers in New York City, and yet, except for an occasional concert or art show, there was no place for them to dance. True, Martha Graham used black dancers in marvelously creative ways, but aside from that, the New York City concert dance scene was basically closed to black dancers. There was practically no way for us to fulfill our compelling desire to participate fully in the dance world. There was no Lester Horton on the East Coast dance scene.

Even against those long odds, I very much wanted to be a choreographer. I had wearied of doing other people's concerts, having done many in the early 1950s after *House of Flowers* closed. I was tired of being told what to do. I had my own ideas, and the time had come for me to make my own decisions. It was common, in those days, for young choreographers to do concerts at the Young Men's Hebrew Association on Ninety-second Street and Lexington Avenue. The YMHA was the hub of modern dance because every night a concert was presented there. The management made it easy for young choreographers, since their work could be performed without costing the YWHA a lot of money. I saw concerts there by Eleo Pomare, Talley Beatty, Donnie McKayle, Pearl Lang, and any number of fine choreographers. These groups would spend about six to eight weeks rehearsing in a dingy little studio called Michael's on Eighth Avenue between Forty-sixth and Forty-seventh Streets, and then they would do a one-performance concert.

My great dream was to pull together a group so I could show the world my work. I had met Ernest Parham when we danced together in *Show Boat*. He was a very intelligent, artistic guy, a former Katherine Dunham dancer, who was then appearing on Broadway in *Bells Are Ringing* with Judy Holiday. (I was dancing on Broadway in *Jamaica* with Lena Horne at the same time.) Ernest was also a choreographer, and we decided to do a concert together. Neither of us was financially or artistically ready to present a full evening of our works, so we decided to share expenses. He pulled together dancers he liked, including some from *Bells Are Ringing,* and I chose an extraordinary group from *Jamaica,* whom I had met in classes and with whom I had danced for Donnie McKayle. Claude Thompson was the lead dancer in my first concert. Other dancers were Charles Moore, Jacqueline Walcott, Clarence Cooper, Lavinia Hamilton, and Audrey Mason, a beautiful dancer who looked like Carmen and in later concerts became my partner. Nancy Redi sang. Ernest brought along Christyne Lawson, Georgia Collins, Ronnie Frazier, and the marvelous Talley Beatty.

Each day for two months, we rehearsed at dingy, dark Michael's Studio from two o'clock in the afternoon until six o'clock. Talley Beatty was often next door to us composing *The Road of the Phoebe Snow.* Then we would grab something to eat and go off to perform the shows we were in, if in fact we were in any. Rehearsal time cost two dollars an hour, and the dancers rehearsed with me for nothing: there was simply no money to pay them.

I decided that my first great contribution to the world as a choreographer would be *Blues Suite,* a dance about the Dew Drop Inn of my Texas childhood. I cast people according to type—Lavinia Hamilton, a stunning woman who looked like every one of those gorgeous black women who danced in the Dew Drop Inn, was cast in that part. Nancy Redi played the role of the woman on the ladder—a character who used to live upstairs from me and my mother and whose boyfriends (and there were many of them) would climb up the stairs to visit her. The ten other characters in the dance represented various aspects of people I remembered from those Texas days.

Geoffrey Holder—we were very close at the time, though we aren't now—designed the costumes for *Blues Suite.* They must have cost all of fifty dollars. We didn't have a penny to spend on anything, so the costumes were made out of women's slips and feathers from the Salvation Army. There was frantic sewing in my living room and backstage as Geoffrey directed everybody to make those costumes. It was a time of sore muscles and angst over the music, and yet, looking back on it, it was a good time. I was constantly looking for the right piece of music; I was constantly on the phone with the designer and wondering whether the dancers were going to come to rehearsal. I'm sure I still owe people money from 1958, most notably a printer who created a beautiful flier for us. Everything in those days of *Blues Suite* was done for nothing—purely out of a regard for the dance. Those were indeed good times.

In *Blues Suite* I felt I was saying something truthful about Texas. And the dancers were terrific; I didn't have to worry about them. I knew they were ready. What concerned me was my choreography. Was it ready for the dreaded scrutiny of New York City audiences and critics? And were they ready for the down-home blackness of *Blues Suite*? As it turned out, they were. John Martin of the *New York Times* described *Blues Suite* as "overflowing with variety, beautifully staged with excellent decor and costumes by Geoffrey Holder and on this occasion was superbly danced." He described me as having "a rich animal quality of movement and an innate sense of theatrical projection."

Dance Magazine said I was "exceptional. [Ailey] reminds one of a caged lion full of lashing power that he can contain or release at will. And perhaps because he is so unusual, he knows instinctively how to compose for other unusual dancers, notably Charles Moore and Clive Thompson." The review described Geoffrey's costumes for *Blues Suite* as "nothing short of breathtaking."

Lena Horne, always supportive, came to that first concert. She had an insider's knowledge of the ballet because several of us were also in *Jamaica,* and we were always doing some of our steps just before the curtain went up on the show. "What are you all doing?" she would ask. "What's going on, Earth Man?" "I'm making a ballet," I told her.

Charles Blackwell, the stage manager for *Jamaica,* also saw the first concert in 1958, and he was soon to become very important to us. When we opened, we didn't have a stage manager to handle rehearsal schedules and a multitude of other details, so Charlie, one of the warmest and most talented people I've ever known, decided that he would be stage manager for the second concert, in 1959. He brought along his good friend Bob Buckalow to help out.

One thing we needed was a better place for rehearsals. Charlie knew of Clark Center. It had once been a famous old hotel and was slated to be made into a senior citizens' center. It was an enormous space with beautiful floors and contained a large ballroom, a little theater, and two other rooms. Clark Center was run by Adele Holtz, who became very important to us. Charlie said he would ask her if we could rehearse there. She came to a rehearsal that night and seemed to fall in love at first sight with what we were doing. She told me, "Yes, you must come and rehearse here." And so we had the use of all that wonderful space. There were no mirrors, true, but Clark Center was a godsend to us poor folk who had no rehearsal home. Every time I pass by it these days, my heart does a little jerk, and my mind is flooded with happy memories.

Miss Holtz attended our second concert at the YMHA and was bowled over. She said, "Oh my God, so *this* is what you're doing!" She decided that Clark Center would not become a senior citizens' center after all; what the neighborhood needed was a performing arts center, a place for the young groups to rehearse and perform. And that's how Clark Center became our home. Ecstasy is the only word to describe my feelings. First thing, we built a room for all the costumes. They had been jammed into my apartment. Now we refashioned a space into a sewing room. We refurbished the theater so that we could give performances there. Miss Holtz's idea was that the group could stay together and take on students, so we established a teaching schedule of classes. Our entire family of performers became a part of Clark Center. It was a lively place, a heaven, a wonderful center, especially for black dancers.

Now that I had a space, I felt a growing urgency to present a full concert of my work, and this time Carmen would be in it. I made a ballet for her called *Arietta Oubliée*. Carmen played the moon, and I played a Marcel Marceau–like character who yearns for the moon. There was also a new version of *Blues Suite*. (I am accustomed to changing things around until I get them right.) Once again, despite all the difficulties—there still was no money—and with a new group of dancers, we put on the concert at the YMHA. We had to adjust rehearsals constantly to fit the dancers' work schedules, and those who were not in a show were working other jobs during the daytime.

Dancers in the second concert, all of them extraordinary, were Ella Thompson, Minnie Marshall, Dorine Richardson, Lavinia Hamilton, Ilene Tema, Clive Thompson, Cliff Fears, Tommy Johnson, Herman Howell, Charles Neal, Charles Moore, Jacqueline Walcott, Carmen, and me.

The concert looked stunning, thanks to my good friend Normand Maxon, who produced it. Normand, who died in 1986, had a colorful history. Short and Jewish, he knew everything there was to know about dance. He had been a dancer, a designer, a painter; he was a true New Yorker. He had a gorgeous apartment on Fifty-fourth Street and ran around with all the hoity-toity, "high" blacks and with the leading musicians and composers in town. He introduced me to a man on Fifty-seventh Street who had a stash of cocaine in his back room; years later that man became my main source of supply, but not until 1979, around the time that Joyce Trisler died.

During *House of Flowers* Normand used to shower me with attention. It's no exaggeration to say that he was absolutely mad about me. When I decided to do another concert, Normand decided to produce it. So this time, instead of having Geoffrey Holder sewing pieces of material from stores on Fourteenth Street, Normand put the full force of his connections and sophistication behind us. We had hats by Oscar de la Renta; we had chiffon dresses for our ritual; we had the most incredible kinds of costumes, all of which Normand made—and always with his hands reaching toward me and me always backing up, saying, "Now, Normand, just do the costumes. You don't have to do me, too." He accepted that with great frustration because, although he loved me, he also loved what I was doing in the theater and wanted to remain a part of it. He made an elaborate set of extraordinary costumes for a dance called *Cinco Latinos,* an imitation of Lester Horton's Latin American dances but with my theme and my style.

Costumes are very important, especially in character dances, and most of my dances are about people. It's also important to have costumes that are elegant, tasteful, artistic, that frame the dancers beautifully—and, more practically, that will endure and be washable. I have always called my company a dance theater because I believe that bringing together the elements of music, costumes, lights, movement, and themes creates a totality that the word *dance* alone does not encompass. Clothes have always been important to me, whether I make them, the dancers make them, or Geoffrey Holder makes them. How the costumes look, how the fabric moves, is very important, and that is why we spend a lot of money on costumes.

Normand was also a photographer, and sometimes on a Saturday our dance theater would go to a studio Normand had access to and he would photograph us dressed in his costumes. He took some wonderful pictures, both in color and black and white, and he designed a wonderful brochure for us. Normand had all the connections; he knew everybody—the printers, the layout people, the color separators. The bare-torso brochure cover of me from the concert in 1959 is a classic of Normand's. He wanted me to live with him and be his lover. But I never felt that way about him.

We did one performance of the *Arietta Oubliée.* One critic said: "Carmen de Lavallade performed the moon with distinction. And Mr. Ailey was appealing as the voyager. But props are no substitute for meaningful dance." About *Blues Suite* it was said: "One of the most satisfying elements of *Blues Suite* is its sense of dramatic pulse—the sure way it contains intensity and languor, irony and sentiment, anguish and impishness. And, throughout, it explores Negro musical idioms—not decoratively, but in an honest life context. Every dancer in Mr. Ailey's large company performed with true identification, and Normand Maxon's flapper costumes were stunning."

Another wrote of *Cinco Latinos*, "Most successful among the adroitly constructed dances were 'El Cigaro,' projected with delicious humor by Charles Moore and Jacqueline Walcott, and 'Rite,' performed with admirable fluid intensity by Alvin Ailey and Audrey Mason as the Initiates."

P. W. Manchester wrote: "After so many modern dance performances in which dancers drift about with blank faces and a general neutralization that denies the existence of sex even in the midst of the most complex entwinings, how refreshing to enter the stage world created by Alvin Ailey in which the men are men and the women are frankly delighted about it."

EIGHT

Revelations

---

*R*evelations began with the music. As early as I can remember I was enthralled by the music played and sung in the small black churches in every small Texas town my mother and I lived in. No matter where we were during those nomadic years Sunday was always a churchgoing day. There we would absorb some of the most glorious singing to be heard anywhere in the world.

With profound feeling, with faith, hope, joy, and sometimes sadness, the choirs, congregations, deacons, preachers, and ushers would sing black spirituals and gospel songs. They sang and played the music with such fervor that even as a small child I could not only hear it but almost see it. I remember hearing "Wade in the Water" being sung during baptism and hearing the pastor's wife sing "I Been 'Buked, I Been Scorned" one Sunday during testifying time. I tried to put all of that feeling into *Revelations.*

My plan was to make *Revelations* the second part of an all-black evening of dance. First would be the blues in *Blues Suite,* then spirituals in *Revelations,* then a section on Kansas City jazz, then a section on contemporary music. The aim was to show the coming and the growth and reach of black culture.

I had also decided that I wanted to develop a black folk dance company that would combine the work of Katherine Dunham and a Filipino dance company I once saw. We would present a concert based on Black American material—songs from the Georgia Sea Islands, New Orleans songs with old blues singers, work songs, folk songs. I planned to do a suite of blues and then a suite of spirituals. *Blues Suite* would be the first part of that.

I did extensive research, listened to a lot of music, dug even deeper into my early Texas memories, and came up with the piece that I would call *Revelations*. I phoned Hall Johnson, a wonderful man who lived uptown, and said, "We want to do this dance two to three months from now from all these spirituals. I would like you to sing." He had a choir and led me to a lot of music, including "I Been 'Buked, I Been Scorned," which I didn't know he had arranged. He decided not to do the concert, and I ended up with a group from the YMCA in Harlem. One way or another, I had to have live music; for me there was no other way.

I divided an hour of these pieces into three sections. First I did it chronologically, leading off with the opening part of *Revelations,* which was the earliest in time. It was about trying to get up out of the ground. The costumes and set would be colored brown, an earth color, for coming out of the earth, for going into the earth. The second part was something that was very close to me—the baptismal, the purification rite. Its colors would be white and pale blue. Then there would be the section surrounding the gospel church, the holy rollers, and all that the church happiness. Its colors would be earth tones, yellow, and black.

At the time I was very involved with the work of the sculptor Henry Moore. (Lester had admired him, too; I guess I picked up my love of Moore from him.) I liked the way Moore's figures were abstracted, stretched, strained, and pulled. His work inspired the costumes made of jersey in the first part of *Revelations*. When the body moves, the jersey takes on extraordinary tensions.

The first version of *Revelations* was quite long, an hour and five minutes, and it had three sections. The first was called "Pilgrim of Sorrow." I took all the songs dealing with black people's sorrow and put them in this section; at the time there were about five or six songs. The middle section was to be wading in the water. Songs such as "Honor, Honor" had all these extraordinary words. I was moved by what spirituals say as words, as metaphors. So I found these short songs for the middle section.

There were quite a few songs for the last section, "Move, Members, Move." The whole ballet was a gigantic suite of spirituals. I poured in just about everything, every beautiful spiritual I had ever heard. From the beginning I thought the first version of *Revelations* might be too long, but nobody ever complained about the length. The critics and audiences had nothing but the most delicious praise from the beginning. We did two concerts in 1960, when *Revelations* was premiered.

Revelations didn't reach its real popularity until it was edited. When we were invited to Jacob's Pillow in 1961 to do an evening of our entire repertoire, I had no music for *Revelations;* it had always been done to live music. But we couldn't afford to take the singers to Jacob's Pillow, so we had to hurriedly come up with taped music. In those days you couldn't just run to a studio, start taping, and come up with something usable. I approached Howard Roberts, a wonderful black choral conductor and an associate at Clark Center; together we took bits and pieces of this and that and put them together in order to be able to take *Revelations* to Jacob's Pillow. I had to make do with the written music we created, so the first section became three pieces instead of six. There was another song after "Rocka My Soul" called "Elijah Rock," a beautiful song about faith. It was my favorite of the two, but the audience liked "Rocka My Soul" better, and that's what they got.

After I snipped, cut, pushed, and pulled *Revelations* down to a half hour, we went off to Jacob's Pillow. Carmen and I did *Roots of the Blues;* Jimmy Truitte and Carmen did Lester Horton's *Beloved;* Carmen and I did Lester Horton's *Orozco;* and a group of five dancers did *Revelations,* which was a huge success and proved to be the hit of the evening. The sequence I settled on was "I Been 'Buked," then "Didn't My Lord Deliver Daniel," "Fix Me, Jesus," the processional, and finally "Wading in the Water." When we went offstage after "Wading in the Water" the audience jumped up and screamed, and they've been jumping and screaming over *Revelations* ever since.

It's pretty clear that there's a love affair between audiences and *Revelations.* The idea of producing spirituals on such a grand scale appealed to everyone. It had beautiful songs sung live by soloists. *Revelations* was long, but people always responded enthusiastically to every song and every movement by the dancers.

When we performed *Revelations* in Athens at the Herod Atticus, an amphitheater with six thousand seats, every one was filled. It was an unforgettable experience to hear that many people screaming for twenty minutes at the curtain. They just loved the music; they were totally into it, and that happens all over the world with this work. We had a big success in Russia, where all the rhythm and hand clapping is an integral part of their folk dances.

The last time we were in Paris five thousand people clapped, stomped, and screamed until we had to do two encores. The Germans and the Italians, too, fell in love with *Revelations.* In fact, we always close with *Revelations* in Europe. I think that the

State Department invited us to go on tour in Southeast Asia in 1962 in part because of the universal popularity of the music in *Revelations*. In Southeast Asia I heard Indonesian music that sounded very much like the blues; I heard Burmese music that sounded very much like spirituals. The French have their spirituals. The tune and texture of the spirituals speak to everybody.

I'm not afraid to say there's not one song in *Revelations* that doesn't hold the listeners' interest. The songs are poetic, and the rhythm that grows out of them is black rhythm. The songs are truthful and a real coming together of music and ideas through dance. The songs also represent a coming together of many things in my head—of youthful energy and enthusiasm, of my concern about projecting the black image properly. They reflect my own feelings about being pressed into the ground of Texas; they re-create the music I heard from ladies in Texas who sold apples while singing spirituals, memories of songs my mother would hum around the house, and the songs I sang in junior high school. We would sing "Rocka My Soul" in my junior high glee club. The songs in *Revelations* are all of those things. And I think they have meant a lot to audiences everywhere.

Church people share a special fondness for *Revelations*, and many of the most devout church people are black; yet despite the success of *Revelations*, we are still trying to get more blacks into the theater. One of the promises of my company is that its repertoire will include pieces that ordinary people can understand. I still dream that my folks down on the farm in Texas can come to an Ailey concert and know and appreciate what's happening onstage. That's my perception of what dance should be—a popular form, wrenched from the hands of the elite.

Black folks now make up roughly twenty percent of our audience, and the percentage should be greater. Many dance promoters, however, don't advertise in the black press. More than once we've run into black people in the streets of a Midwestern city who ask, "Who are you?" because they know we don't live there. We explain that we're a dance company at the theater down the street. As I say, that scene has been repeated more than once, and it will take very sophisticated marketing to achieve our aim of bringing more black people into the theater.

About fifteen or twenty years ago, when we were setting out on a European tour, I said, "I want to stop taking this piece to Europe." I made up my mind to leave *Revelations* home. But after two performances the dancers and audiences were asking, "Where's *Revelations*?" and of course we had to relent. It was so popular a piece that it was dangerous to lead off a performance with it. Once we did it first on a program, everybody went home after it was over. Even after all these years, we still feel that our season at New York City Center, where we play for four weeks, hasn't really begun until we do *Revelations*. If we open on a Wednesday and *Revelations* isn't presented until Sunday, the stage somehow hasn't yet been blessed.

As for me, though, I'm more interested in what's next. Sometimes I don't want to hear another word about this thirty-year-old dance, and I decided that after our thirtieth anniversary in 1988, I would put *Revelations* away for a while.

NINE

The Group's First Tour of Australia, Southeast Asia, and Brazil

---

$\mathcal{W}$hen we were invited, in 1962, to make our first tour to Southeast Asia, we were still a group and not yet formally organized as a company. I don't believe you can call yourself a company until you have enough money to keep your dancers alive. Dancers were always coming and going, and at the end of each concert maybe three or four would remain out of ten or twelve. People such as Thelma Hill, Nat Horne, and Harold Pierson would often work even when there was no money coming in.

The dancers who went on the Asian tour were those whose work I had seen and appreciated over the years. I first saw Minnie Marshall at a concert in downtown Manhattan; I first saw Thelma Hill when she was dancing with another ballet company; I first saw Georgia Collins doing Talley Beatty's *Road of the Phoebe Snow*. Don Martin and Jimmy Truitte were both from Los Angeles, and both had danced with the Lester Horton group. Charles Moore, another dancer in our tour, didn't have much technique, but he was a brilliant natural dancer.

Originally, the tour was to begin in India earlier in the year, but the countries got involved in a war with Pakistan, and the U.S. State Department switched us quickly to Australia. We opened in Sydney. They had booked us into a theater called the Palace, a wonderful old-fashioned space that seated about 1,100 people. When we got there, nobody had the foggiest notion of who we were. The State Department had booked us on the spur of the moment, with no advance publicity. We had to explain that we were the de Lavallade-Ailey Dance Theater, the name we were touring under. When we opened in Sydney, the theater was virtually empty; maybe twenty-five people came the first night. We did *Been Here and Gone;* Carmen did *Beloved;* Carmen and I did *Roots of the Blues;* and we did *Revelations.* The twenty-five or so people in attendance went absolutely mad. The next day when we arrived at rehearsal at two o'clock in the afternoon, there were many people in the streets near the theater who had read the newspapers and were lined up to get tickets. The newspapers said we were fabulous and told people they'd better get there at once to see us.

The second might we performed, there wasn't an empty seat in the house. The audience screamed, hollered, and stomped. The critics said that Carmen was the most beautiful woman in the world and I was one of the handsomest men. Carmen and I were stretching ourselves to the limit, and Brother John Sellers was singing beautifully. I had met Brother John in 1959 when I was doing Saroyan's *Talking to You.* I used to go through Washington Square Park in Greenwich Village to get to the subway, and one day I passed by this club called Folk City and heard a voice singing "Every Evening When the Sun Goes Down," one of my favorite blues songs. I said to myself, "Who the hell is that *singing?*" I started stopping by the club all the time to listen to Brother John sing. He was a Mississippian who sang the blues with real dirt in his voice, with such wonderful grit. I finally got to know him. I told him that I wanted to do a dance called *Roots of the Blues,* and I would love to have him sing for me. We got it together and have been close friends ever since.

After Sydney we traveled down to Melbourne. They had no legitimate theater to put us in, so we were booked into a huge 3,500-seat movie theater where *The Sound of Music* was playing. We opened at five o'clock in the afternoon, just when people were getting off work. As had happened in Sydney, approximately twenty-five attended our first performance and over three thousand the next day.

There was no question that they loved us in Australia. The Aussies had never seen anything like this—ten black dancers doing their thing with grace, great music, and professional savvy. They screamed from beginning to end; there was thunderous applause that went on and on, people throwing flowers, people crying. It was our first taste of performing before large audiences who liked us with no reservations. The critics also liked us, and best of all, we got paid every week. We left there very happy and professionally fulfilled.

Our next stop was Burma, where we performed in a theater near the Shwedagon Pagoda. When we did our first ballet, a piece called *Been Here and Gone,* we ran downstage and there was no applause. Thelma Hill yelled, "Go back. Go back. Dim the lights." We thought, "This is awful. They hate us." After one more piece, which also drew no applause, a State Department official explained to us that the Burmese never respond by clapping their hands. In the Burmese culture, silence is the way you show your appreciation. Burma (thank God!) was the only country where we received no applause.

Over a period of three months we played in Australia, Burma, Malaya, Japan, Hong Kong, South Korea, Indonesia, and Vietnam. When we weren't performing, we ate exotic meals, attended receptions, visited every music school in Southeast Asia, heard every children's chorus, met every head of a music school and every mayor in every village. Martha Graham had toured Southeast Asia for the State Department before us, but we were the first to tour so extensively. She toured only the big cities; we went everywhere, no matter how small the town.

This tour established a strong connection between us and the Japanese people. We traveled through the country, and the Japanese absolutely fell in love with us. At that time what we were doing was new to them. The dirt and grit of *Revelations* and *Blues Suite* and the power of Brother John's singing had a profound impact on audiences all over Southeast Asia but especially so in Japan. Because we were there under the auspices of the State Department, we were always going to parties and various government functions. Two members of the company— musician Bruce Langhorne and one of my dancers, Georgia Collins—got married in Japan in the ambassador's garden in Tokyo. We did not return to Japan until the late 1970s; since then we've been going there every other year. The Japanese always come to our City Center season to see what's new and what we will bring to them the season after that. They are very close to us.

When we first toured Vietnam, the war had not yet started, but American soldiers were already stationed there. But not in uniform. Everyone in the military wore civilian clothes. A lot of American kids with butch haircuts were walking around in army shoes and flowered shirts. We performed in Saigon, in an area called Chu-Lon, the Chinese section of town. There were about thirty people in the theater, and they sat spread far apart because at the time the city was under a siege of terrorism. Public places were being bombed. (We discovered this *after* we got there.) We were staying in an old French hotel called the Majestic, and at night we could hear gunfire in the distance. We woke up one morning and found an aircraft carrier loaded with airplanes sitting right next to the hotel. We decided it was time to move on.

Indonesia—there's no other way to say this—was a dreadful experience. There was no air conditioning anywhere—not in the hotels where we stayed, not in the theater. In the hotels the sheets were dirty; everything was filthy. But we danced. That was the important thing. We danced the very best we could. For three months I had a group of people who danced together, and got paid, and I couldn't have been prouder of that group of soulful, personable, very talented, wonderful people. No matter how rough the conditions were, the dancers looked absolutely stunning—tall, gorgeous black women and striking, handsome black men. When we returned from Southeast Asia, though, the group fell apart. Unfortunately, we were still not a company, since we were back to operating without funds.

While casting around for my next move, I taught workshops and dance technique at Connecticut College in New London. Watch Hill, Rhode Island, was about an hour away, and the Joffrey Ballet was there, housed in Rebekah Harkness's fifty-two-room summer place. The Joffrey's general manager, Gerald Arpino, picked me up every day after my classes and drove me to Watch Hill. I would rehearse there all afternoon; then he would drive me back to New London. I made a ballet for them called *Feast of Ashes*.

In 1963, I met Duke Ellington. He was putting together a show called *My People* for the observance of the one hundredth anniversary of the Emancipation Proclamation. He had heard about me and *Revelations* and came to see the ballet. He fell in love with it. He especially liked "I Been 'Buked" and all its hand movements. When he asked me if my group would consider being a part of his show, I was ecstatic. I didn't know until later that he had assigned two choreographers to do the numbers in his show, Talley Beatty and me. He also assigned us to choreograph the same pieces of music. He showed me the steps he wanted me to do, and I happily accepted the challenge. We did the blues for *Black, Brown, and Beige;* Talley did a brilliant piece for the brass.

We rehearsed *My People* in Chicago. Duke was always getting ideas, and I had a few of my own. I told him that I would love to do a duet if he would write me a Stravinskyesque piece about three minutes long. So one morning at about five o'clock he woke me out of a sound sleep and said, "Alvin, this is Duke. I finished the duet. Come over about noon and I'll play it for you." He had written a gorgeous duet with strings for me and Minnie Marshall.

Talley was beginning to cause problems. He was a brilliant man but very temperamental. Duke had assigned him a number of responsibilities in connection with the show, but when Talley got involved in his ballet he was a perfectionist and incapable of concentrating on other things. With the situation growing tense, I said to Duke, with whom I had gotten friendly, "You can't do all this by yourself, the staging, the scenery, writing the music, conducting the orchestra." "I can do it," he said, but in fact he was being unrealistic. Reluctantly, I started staging things when he wasn't there. I ended up helping him stage the whole show. After he saw that I had some talent for staging, he let me help him in any way I saw fit. When people would ask him, "Duke, what about this? What about that?" he would defer to me, saying, "Ask Alvin," which I thought was a great compliment.

Duke and I got to be rather friendly. We talked a lot, about everything under the sun. At that time he had a special friend, a Belgian countess, who was just wonderful. She had a fabulous collection of jewelry and dresses, and she followed him everywhere. You couldn't look in his mouth without her looking too. She even followed him into the bathroom. Duke and I got some laughs out of that.

After the Ellington show closed, I had to rehearse what was basically a new group of performers for a music festival in Rio de Janeiro and São Paulo. I put together another version of *Been Here and Gone,* with African singers and songs, and a new version of *Roots of the Blues* for Myrna White and me. She had been brought in from New York City because Carmen had other commitments and wouldn't be going with us. Of course, we were also going to do *Revelations.* Brother John, like Carmen, had prior commitments, and so Lou Gossett was with us to sing the blues numbers.

By this time I had hired a black man, Ben Jones, to manage the company. He had set up the Brazil tour. The night *My People* closed in Chicago, I was trying, despite a fever of 104 degrees, to pull together all the ballets we would be performing in Brazil and to find costumes. We flew to New York City, picked up some musicians waiting at the airport, and flew on to Rio. We arrived there, exhausted, around two o'clock in the afternoon. Our first performance was advertised for eight o'clock that same evening. You can imagine our shock and dismay when we arrived at the theater to discover that it was locked tight. There was nobody to be found anywhere to open the doors. It took us an hour and a half to find the festival people. We finally got into the theater around four o'clock, only to discover orchestra instruments scattered all over the stage. More time was spent trying to find somebody to give the theater a semblance of order.

Our concert had been advertised simply as the Ballet Alvin Ailey—no elaboration. When the curtain went up for the first ballet, *Been Here and Gone,* a piece dealing with the coming of Africans to America, all of us standing there in African clothing with drums playing, the Brazilian audience gasped. These people were dressed to within an inch of their lives, some wearing emeralds as big as pigeon eggs. They had thought we were a traditional ballet company, and evidently they were shocked when they saw all of us black people shaking our behinds.

The show was just a so–so success. I was angry and frustrated because everything seemed to go wrong. Lou Gossett forgot the words to the songs; the curtain didn't work; the sound was off; some of the costumes fell off. It was horrible, and I was really livid. You have never heard a nigger scream so much backstage in your life. In those days when I got mad I would race around and snatch each dressing-room door open, ream out whoever was inside very loudly, and then slam the door. "You call that *dancing?*" I screamed. "That's nothing, absolutely nothing!" *Bam!* would go the door. I told Lou Gossett to catch the next flight home. I was especially furious with him because he had not only forgotten the words, but also was singing off-key. It was terrible, horrible.

We traveled from Rio to São Paulo. Thank God, we were more successful there. We met many wonderful black people in São Paulo who were involved in the folk heritage of Brazil and who traveled up and down the Amazon River. Knowing them helped to ease the pain of the disaster in Rio, but our situation was still far from perfect. We didn't get enough rehearsal time, a common problem in the early days of touring. Nothing was ever really right except the performances themselves.

Something good did happen in Rio, though. In the middle of all my screaming at the cast and the Gods came a knock on my door from a man named Dr. Benjamin Kean. He was a specialist in tropical medicine who was married to Rebekah Harkness, a billionairess. He asked me to begin research for a ballet she wanted to do about Brazil. He also gave me, as I recall, one thousand dollars to go to El Salvador and buy some sculpture for her. So when the company went back to New York City, I went to El Salvador and spent a week looking at dances and having a good time. I guess you could call that trip one of the perquisites of an uncertain profession.

TEN

Giants

Now I will talk about giants I have known—those important figures in theater and dance and music whose powerful personalities have left marked impressions on me. First of all, Pearl Bailey. Shortly before I arrived as a fledgling dancer for *House of Flowers,* the director, Peter Brooks, had said something to the cast that they interpreted as blatantly racist. Pearl Bailey, in particular, had taken great offense. She had stopped speaking to him. In the process of rehearsing a show the last thing you need is a war between star and director, but, at the time, Miss Bailey was a very uptight, arrogant, lady—perpetually on her high horse—and as the star of the show she rarely spoke to anybody. She would stride around the theater—gorgeous, tall, imposing, and somber. I can't say that I ever really got to know her well. Later in the show, when Brooks had been replaced and the tension had abated, Pearl Bailey became friendly with the dancers and revealed her sense of humor.

What impressed me most about Bailey and other giants in the arts was their awesome knowledge of their craft. Pearl Bailey had been in show business longer than I had lived. She and Lena Horne knew everything about booking; they knew about musical arrangements; they knew about costumes and scenery design. They could walk out onstage and make the most astute remarks about what was going on at any moment. I once saw Lena Horne conduct an orchestra. It was cold in the theater, I remember; she had on a robe, and her head was wrapped in a turban. As she stood on the stage, singing, she stopped the orchestra every fifteen bars and said, "No, no, that's not it. I want it to go like this."

Lena is the sweetest and most adorable woman in the world. When I was rehearsing for my first concert, she was very encouraging, saying again and again, "You're going to be a wonderful choreographer, Alvin." She still supports my company by doing galas to help raise money. She not only has beauty but also strength and wisdom. She's a real black woman. It amazed me to see Lena in action and to watch black women like her—Pearl Bailey, Katherine Dunham, Claudia McNeil, and Josephine Premice—deal with the world. They are all very wise, very strong, and so beautiful to look at. They are also tough. Miss Dunham, listening to our orchestra at City Center through her dressing-room door, heard the overture being played slightly off-key. Dead serious, she said, "They're not playing my music well, Alvin. They are off because they don't warm up. Fire them!"

I saw the same attitude in such peers as Diana Sands and Cicely Tyson, but it was less marked in them than in the star personalities. Lesser stars have a way of subduing themselves when there are ladies around like Claudia McNeil or Pearl Bailey. Those women are such forces. When you're working in a play with McNeil or Bailey, you are not the Diva for the Day.

A Leontyne Price story illustrates how a giant speaks when she has to make herself understood. It happened when we were rehearsing *Anthony and Cleopatra,* for the inaugural of the new Metropolitan Opera House at Lincoln Center. Thomas Schippers was the conductor, I was the choreographer, Franco Zefferelli was director, Sam Barber was the composer. Every morning on her way to rehearsals the great Miss Price would come by to see what the dancers were doing. Like Lena Horne and Pearl Bailey, she liked to watch the dancers. Sometimes she would sit for forty-five minutes watching us sweat. Mr. Zefferelli would come in, run up to her, embrace her, and say, "Madame! Madame! Surely this is the voice for whom Verdi wrote *Aida.*" She would say, "Thank you, Maestro." They would go kiss-kiss-kiss, and he would rush off to his directorial chores.

About ten days before opening, Miss Price came in and was not in a happy mood. Her mouth was turned down; she was really furious as she sat in the chair watching us. When Mr. Zefferelli came in and said, "Madame! Madame!" Miss Price cut in, saying, " 'Madame,' my ass. You'd better come in and rehearse my scenes. I've got to open this opera house up in ten days." He had been doing everything but her stuff. That afternoon there was a big red pencil line through all rehearsal schedules. The rest of the day was devoted to Miss Leontyne Price and to her only.

And there was the fabulous Duke. When, as a teenager in the 1940s, I first came across Duke Ellington, his "Take the A Train" and "Satin Doll" were very popular. I used to see this amazing-looking man in a white suit with slicked-back hair sitting at a white piano in the Lincoln Theater, which was in a black neighborhood, and in the Orpheum Theater in a white neighborhood—both were in Los Angeles. The band members also dressed in white suits as they played his gorgeous music. That was when I began to worship him from afar.

I met him for the first time in 1963 when he asked me to be

in his show *My People*. About seven years later the question came up about my doing a ballet for the American Ballet Theater, then headed by Lucia Chase. She said, "Alvin, I've got a ballet for you to make. You and Duke Ellington. We must have the two of you." When she put her mind to something, you had to go along because she was a force of nature.

She sent me to Vancouver, British Columbia, where Duke was playing. I flew all night and arrived in time to see his eleven o'clock show that evening. Everybody was in black tuxedos. I watched as Duke kissed people who were recently married and sang "Happy Birthday" to people celebrating their birthdays. He was completely charming. After the show I went backstage and found him lying on a couch, his do-rag wrapped around his hair. (He loved his hair.) All the musicians were wandering in and out of his room, and he was ministering to them like some kind of emir. He told me that we could talk after the second show.

When the night's work was finally done, this glossy creature with the deeply lined face, this wise man who moments before, dressed in his satin tuxedo, had charmed everyone in sight, put on his regular clothes, and we crept up the hill to his hotel, a place called the Cave, to talk. No longer onstage, where he radiated a kind of perpetual youth, he became a seventy-year-old man.

Duke asked me if I wanted a drink. When I said that I would, he took about ten little bottles of liquor out of an airline bag, made me a drink (he didn't touch alcohol), and we began talking. I told him that I wanted to do a kind of rhapsodic ballet.

But Duke had another idea. President Nixon had given Duke a seventy-first-birthday celebration at the White House and presented him with a citation. Duke said, "Everything would've been just fine if they hadn't given me that citation. Now everybody knows how old I am." He was very upset about that. He told me a story about a king who couldn't laugh, couldn't smile. The king's court did everything to make him laugh, but he just couldn't crack a smile. The queen tried; the best juggler in the world tried; the court jesters tried. They did all these numbers for the king—he was really talking about Nixon—but he still wouldn't laugh. Finally, one of the clowns brought the king a mirror. When he looked in the mirror, he cracked up. The way Duke told the story was very theatrical—moving and funny.

Then he started talking about a ballet called *The River,* which was to be a suite of dances based on water, with a line about life that goes from birth to death. As we talked, he began to play the music. At five o'clock in the morning I was sitting in Duke Ellington's apartment bathed in beautiful music. I said, "Let's do it. Let's do *The River.*" There were to be nine or ten sections to the ballet, but only about eight ever got done.

After we agreed to a collaboration, he was gone all of the time. I had about three weeks to do the choreography, and the music would arrive page by page. I would make changes, and the next day Duke would send the music back with slight variations. When you have a big group of dancers, you have to be precise. I told Lucia Chase to tell Duke that I didn't want a page of music: I wanted a whole piece. But he continued touring all over, writing music and sending it to me piece by piece. Finally, I told Miss Chase, "I can't do this. I can't work like this." At that very moment the door opened and in walked Duke in a big beige coat and a white hat, looking as though everything were absolutely fine. He said, "If you stopped worrying about the music and started worrying about the choreography, you'd be a lot better off." I said, "What can I do without music?" He said, "Do sixteen bars here and I'll figure it out." I said, "Duke, I can't work like that."

He went away again and continued to send me music, but I

didn't finish the ballet on schedule—you have to have rehearsal time. Still, we performed the sections I had done; the next year I added more music. *The River* still lives. It has beautiful music and is performed all over the world. Unfortunately, Duke died before he had a chance to see it.

The next time I saw Duke was shortly before his death. I had gone to Toronto, where he was playing, to discuss a new project for the two of us. I had a room right down the hall from him. He had done major research on water music and had gathered together every piece of music with a water reference you could think of. He would play something for me on an electric piano and ask if I liked it. His calls to me at four o'clock in the morning became a ritual. He would say, "Hey, Alvin, you ready to work?" He liked to work from four-thirty until seven o'clock in the morning. Then he would go to bed and sleep until three or four in the afternoon. He would tinker again on the piano before getting dressed up, looking for all the world like Big Daddy, and going down to orchestra rehearsal. He stayed there until six-thirty; then he would go back upstairs. The first show started about nine o'clock. At eight his room would be full of sixty-year-old ladies, probably Canadian, whom he called girls. "I don't know what I'm going to do with all these girls," he would say. They just adored him. The shows were at nine and eleven, and during the interval between shows he would party with the ladies.

As giants go, Duke Ellington was one of the largest and grandest of them all.

I met Robert Joffrey, another giant, in 1956 after doing a ballet called *Miss Julie* for a little modern dance company. Nobody in New York knew me as a choreographer at that time, but Anna Sokolow asked me to do a ballet for her company; it turned out to be a very effective little dramatic ballet, and Robert Joffrey, who saw everything in town, was there. He got in touch with me in 1960, about four years later, and said that his company was going to have a workshop at Rebekah Harkness's Watch Hill, Rhode Island, summer house; he was looking for choreographers to work with them while they were there. We agreed that for a six-week period we would make ballets in Watch Hill and see how the chemistry worked between us. I choreographed *Feast of Ashes,* a ballet based on a García Lorca poem. It was during that period that I got to know Joffrey quite well as a man of taste and an awesome knowledge of the history of ballet. He was of Afghan descent—his real name was Abdullah Anver Bey Kahn—and a special bond developed between my blackness and his Afghan-ness. We called him the Little Colonel. Whenever Joffrey walked into the room everybody got up and started doing tendus, an exercise designed to strengthen the ankles and feet. He cared deeply and honestly about other people, and maybe especially about black people. Christian Holder and Gary Christ were members of his company long before any other ballet company even thought about putting Arthur Mitchell anywhere. But Joffrey was not your usual artist. He was an elitist, and he lived the life of a traditional, old-fashioned, artistic gentleman in Greenwich Village, in a carriage house filled with wonderful antiques.

Sometime in 1955, while dancing in *House of Flowers,* I got a message from Geoffrey Holder or Carmen de Lavallade—I can't remember which—saying that Carl Van Vechten wanted me to call him. Van Vechten, a white man who collected black culture, had been deeply involved with the Harlem Renaissance. He wanted to take pictures of me. I was honored, since he had photographed everyone from Bessie Smith to Paul Robeson in the living room of his elegant apartment on Central Park West.

One day, after a composition class with Doris Humphrey, I went to Van Vechten's apartment. He took a series of pictures of me in everything from African fashions to jeans. Many of these pictures are still around in private collections and in some of his books.

Van Vechten was a very warm and gracious party giver. Early in our friendship I was invited to one of his parties to meet a tiny Danish lady named Isak Dinesen, whose birthday it was and about whom I knew nothing. When I walked into the room, she was sitting in a huge chair—a tiny, birdlike creature whose head was wrapped in a turban. She wore masses of pearls, and a kind of glow emanated from her. Finally everybody gravitated to the feet of this lady, and she was introduced as the Countess Blixen, a good friend of Van Vechten's. She talked for about an hour, discussing her book *Out of Africa* and philosophizing about the world. At another party, to celebrate Van Vechten's seventy-fifth birthday, Leontyne Price suddenly began singing "Happy Birthday" to him. He and his wife, ballerina Fania Marinoff, were extraordinary people.

Arnold Saint-Subber, the producer of *House of Flowers,* who had become one of my fans, was a great friend of Carson McCullers. He knew that I admired her, and one day he invited me to dinner at his home to meet her. After dinner she wanted to go to Manhattan's West Side, so the three of us took a cab over to Eighth Avenue and Fifty-second Street. Saint-Subber left us there, and we began strolling along together. Miss McCullers was fascinated by an amusement center on the corner of Fifty-second and Broadway. She stood looking intensely at one of the guys who worked there, a strange young man with stringy blond hair. She said he reminded her of Ross, her lover who had killed himself. Miss McCullers also told me that she was writing a story about somebody who was searching for a black sailor with blue eyes as a kind of symbol of seeking what one cannot achieve. As we walked, she talked about life in the city, about the people of the city, of how the city felt to someone who lived upstate, in

Nyack, New York. McCullers in person, as in her work, was truly a giant.

My view of another giant—George Balanchine—is an outsider's view, because I never really knew him. I first became aware of his name when I was a child in the mid-1940s, and I discovered the Ballet Russe de Monte Carlo on a school trip to the Los Angeles Philharmonic Auditorium. I'm sure that I saw his name in a program, and I probably was aware of his work. By the time I arrived in New York in 1954 to appear in *House of Flowers,* Balanchine had been replaced as choreographer by Herbert Ross, and it was he who brought Carmen and me into the show. Balanchine's choreography for the show was very, very good; it was a kind of neoclassical mambo and had some wonderful staging, but it didn't have enough commercial bump and grind. I think that's why he was replaced.

Balanchine has had an enormous influence on American dancing, especially classical dance. His accomplishments as a choreographer were monumental. I think my professional life really came together when I encountered Balanchine's *Apollo,* which was first performed in 1928. Balanchine was probably the greatest neoclassical choreographer of all time. His background in Russia; his creations with Danilova; his encounter with Lincoln Kirstein, who brought him to America; his creativity; his sensitivity to music and to form and to the American energy— all of those facets, brought together in a man of genius, gave us a new vision of classic dance. It was classic dance with a verve, a new kind of athleticism, a new kind of physical length—Balanchine was very fond of long bodies. There's the Balanchine look—long legs, superbly arched feet, a short torso, long arms, a small head (we call it a peanut head), and a long neck. This physical type, which Balanchine absolutely loved, became the gold standard of classic American dance. But where does that leave our black girls, whose feet are not always so arched and whose torso is not so short? Well, it leaves them out in the cold.

I, too, have a certain kind of dancer that I love. Like Balanchine, I'm attracted to long-legged girls with long arms and a little head, but I also like little, short, fat girls who can turn fast. Black body types are varied, as are all body types, and I like to use them all.

In recent years there have been some black male artists working under Balanchine. Arthur Mitchell became a star with the New York City Ballet. There was one female dancer, Debra Austin, who was with him for a long time. I must say, though, that I think his failure to use more black dancers was probably racially motivated. If you live in the elite world of dance, you find yourself in a world rife with racism. Let's face it: How many black people do you see at high society parties or with the Fords or the DuPonts or whoever makes up the Social Register? There's a deep fault line of racism built into that society because of what it is.

Balanchine's contributions as a teacher, as the founder of a great school, the School of American Ballet, however, are enormous. His school preserves the choreography of Marius Petipa and Michel Fokine, which was a part of Balanchine's roots in Leningrad. With the help of Stanley Williams he also incorporated the style of Auguste Bournonville into his own, recognizing that it was a method that could add to his dancers' virtuosity. It's precisely the kind of thing I'm trying to do with our school. We preserve the Horton technique, the Graham technique, the Dunham technique, so that these ways of moving will not be lost—built upon but not lost.

Balanchine has given the world so much. He influenced me as a choreographer, and he has influenced generations of modern dancers. He taught us how to perceive music in a new way, how to make music visual. He taught a tradition by bringing Russia with him to the United States; he brought all of his 1930s experience with him, as well as his startling gift of creativity, which was probably at that time at its peak.

If I have any criticism of Balanchine, it would be that the idea of this kind of Russian ballet, of this kind of company, the New York City Ballet, is old-fashioned. It's cold. It's unfeeling. The coldness I sense in it is related to music and not to feeling; it's a visual display designed in musical terms. His scores were adventurous and avant-garde; he looked at music like a musician, as figures on a page. Most choreography, no matter what you are trying to say, is attached strongly to the music, but the dancers, I feel strongly, need to be more than the sum of the music; there must be passion, and the dancers must dance that passion. Balanchine wanted his dancers not to show anything on their faces but just become the music itself. I disagree with that approach; I think it dehumanizes dancers. That's something that always bothers me about performances of the New York City Ballet or any of Balanchine's ballets. I like personalities onstage; he liked instruments.

I met Balanchine only once, at the home of Karin von Aroldingen, a dancer in the New York City Ballet, of whom he was very fond. He would go to her and her husband's home and cook. He loved to cook. I spent a very pleasant evening at dinner with Balanchine talking about everything under the sun. He told me about his early life in Russia, about living there through the Russian Revolution and then escaping to Paris. He had seen some of my work, but we didn't talk about it; if he had hated it, I don't think he would have said so. We just talked as choreographers, and I felt he had about him the air of a priest. He was a wonderful, complex man, a very spiritual man, deeply rooted in the old traditions of goodness, joy, good food, good wine, and gorgeous women. He had a really solid philosophy about people.

Talley Beatty—another of my giants—is a great genius.

There are so many things about his work that I like. It's inventive, it's traditional, it's street, it's of the people, it's sophisticated, it's always of the moment—you might say it's everything at once, an amalgam of a whole era of dance styles. He's very involved with black people and their feelings. When he did *The Stack-Up*, he spent most of his time in Harlem. He used to say at rehearsals, "I want this to be like those people walking on 147th Street when they're coming home from work." Images like that, combined with a fine dance vocabulary derived from Dunham, early jazz, Balanchine, and his own inventions, made for explosive work. He was also a brilliant, brilliant dancer. It was Talley, along with Donnie McKayle, who pushed me toward the exploring of my own blackness. They worked in different ways. Talley's is an explosive, energetic vision of choreography; Donnie's is more contemplative, more lyrical.

Dudley Williams is another extraordinary dancer. First of all, he's fifty years old and he's still dancing. He's in great shape and wants to dance another fifty years. Dudley is a very bright man whose strength, like Nureyev's, is his belief in his performance. Five years ago we all said to Dudley, "Well, Dudley, you're now forty-five. How long is this going to go on?" He answered, "Forever. I want to dance." He comes alive when he's onstage. His resolve is incredible—he works, he warms up, he goes to class, he is constantly perfecting his interpretations. He's amazing—an inspiration to everybody, a real poet with movement.

In 1965, I attended an audition Donnie McKayle was holding for a television show, *The Stolen Twenties,* he was going to choreograph for Harry Belafonte. Judith Jamison, whom I didn't know and had never seen before, was one of many girls doing barre exercises for the audition. She looked rather plain in black leotards and tights beside the other girls, who were all made up in lipstick, eyeliner, and all the rest. I couldn't help but notice her, especially the length of the legs, the *feet,* that *back,* those *arms,* that *hair.* I knew immediately that she was someone very special. She wasn't taken for the show, but I decided to find out who she was. It turned out that she was living with Carmen de Lavallade, so I called and asked her to join the company. It took five years before I could really work with Judy, and even though I made a lot of ballets for her through the years, it seemed that we were always in a state of conflict. To put it plainly, Judy couldn't stand me at the beginning, and I couldn't stand her. She did the steps, but there was a separation, a distance. She was shy, she didn't get my message, she was argumentative in rehearsals. "What are you listening to in this music?" she asked. "Da-da-da," I said. "There's no da-da-da there," she insisted. She was snappy until I made *Cry.* That did it; that was the work that broke the ice between us. We began to move toward each other.

And, yes, she, too, proved to be one of the giants in my life.

ELEVEN

Sacrifice, Dancers, Budgets, Race, and Other Things

*O*ver the years I have been obsessed with our dance company. During every waking minute, everything I do somehow revolves around the company; it's all-engrossing. I sacrificed everything to stay in dance—and dance requires enormous sacrifice. The touring, for example. Touring six months out of the year has a fatal effect on personal relations. I don't go all of the time anymore, but I'm a veteran of the tour, having done it for fifteen years.

There is also a physical sacrifice involved in my world. Dancing hurts. After doing a performance, you wake up with cramps at four o'clock in the morning. You don't make much money. You have to be obsessed with dance to do dance; it's not something you play with. The commitment must be there, and the involvement total. As a choreographer, I'm always thinking about the next dance. In my mind's eye I see these figures going across the stage. The creative process is not controlled by a switch you can simply turn on or off; it's with you all the time. For me, choreography is very difficult to do. It's both mentally and physically draining, and one wants to be physically drained by it. In the days when I was in terrific shape and we used to do intricate steps and hard falls on the floor during rehearsals, I felt terrific.

Choreography, as I have said, is also mentally draining, but there's a pleasure in getting into the studio with the dancers and the music and coming out with something that has passion and joy, that shows off the dancers and how they physically reflect the music. There's a kind of joy in creating something where before there was nothing. That keeps me going.

I am very fond of dancers. I like their personalities, I like who they are—their spirit, their physicality, their creativity, their yearning to be perfect. I look for dancers who have something unusual about them physically—a special turn of the leg, a special stretch of the back. I look for dancers who have rubato in their bodies. I believe that dance is not what you do from one movement to the next, it's what happens in between those two movements with the body. I look for dancers who have an oozy quality in their movement. I like dancers who are temperamental, who are expressive, who show their feelings, who are open and out, not hidden, who want to show themselves to the audience. I like personalities, not cookie-cutter dancers—a row of this, a row of that. That's what I accuse Balanchine of: making everyone who dances for him blank-faced.

Dancers these days must also have technique—classical, modern, and jazz. My earlier dancers were not the world's greatest technicians. None of those girls were about to turn forty-two fouettés on a dime, but they had a funk; they had a stride; they had history; they had a menace about them that the young kids don't have today. Today's kids are very technical. They can do eighteen pirouettes on a dime and get their leg way above the head and hold it there. But the insight is not the same: It's not as giving, not as warm. They need to give themselves to the dance, to project themselves from the inside out. That's what we get after them about.

We coach and direct them to bring out their personalities. We want them to be capable of acting out various parts, to become the different individuals in each ballet. That's where personality comes in. It even took talented dancers like Judy Jamison and Donna Wood time and practice to become secure enough physically to let go and truly be themselves. But when you suddenly find yourself in contact with the audience—and it can take years—the result is extraordinary. I saw that happen with Judy; she didn't come on in an extraordinary way with audiences until *Cry*. Her shyness hurt her, but with *Cry* she became herself. Once she found this contact, this release, she poured her being into everybody who came to see her perform. She grew to another level, went on to Broadway, and now has her own dance company.

The question of dance and race is an ever-present one. Look at the problem in England right now. There are black dancers in the Royal Ballet School, but the RBS doesn't want them, so as a result the really good black dancers with potential are sent to Arthur Mitchell's school. The Royal Ballet has an arrangement with Arthur to take them and nurture them so they don't have to deal with all those young black artists. You still don't see many black dancers in classical companies. The Europeans are more open than the Americans. (Maurice Béjart has three black dancers, for example.) In American companies, though, there is still an overlay of racism. I remember in 1966 when my company was going through one of its periodic dissolutions, some of our very top, fantastic dancers—Judith Jamison, Morton Winston, and Miguel Godreau—were invited to the Harkness Ballet. All had terrible times; when it came to utilizing their fantastic abilities, Harkness simply didn't have a clue.

Here, in short, is the big problem with white ballet companies: Does one really want to see a black swan among thirty-two swans in *Swan Lake* or a black peasant girl in *Giselle?* It's historically inaccurate, is the line taken by many of those in charge. Agnes de Mille used that argument with black dancers, and I'll never forgive her for it. When she was holding auditions for a Texas musical, *Ninety Degrees in the Shade,* I believe, she told the black dancers who came to the audition that they were historically inappropriate and refused to hire them.

I give no credence to that position whatsoever. What we're talking about here is dance. Were' talking about fantasy, not reality. We're in the theater, not in a history seminar. It's the same as saying that Japanese dancers can't dance the blues—well, they do in *my* company. Japanese dancers understand the blues as well as anybody. When I began using them and some white dancers in *Blues Suite* and *Revelations,* I got flack from some black groups who resented it. They felt anyone not black was out of place. I received many letters in protest. My answer was that their presence universalizes the material.

My first Japanese-American dancer was the wonderfully talented Mari Kajiwara. When we went to Japan everybody wanted to speak Japanese with her, but she didn't know one word of Japanese. I've also had two memorable male dancers, Masazumi Chaya and Michihiko Oka. Chaya is now ballet master for the AAADT and helps to keep the ballets together. He's a wonderful artist who danced with the company for ten years. Michihiko also danced with the company for ten or twelve years. So our relationship with the Japanese is as close as it is rare.

It goes back to Lester Horton, who was an influence on me in so many ways. When I was with him, he was very involved with the Japanese community in Los Angeles and had a couple of Japanese dancers. I believe there's something in the Japanese aesthetic that is totally black. The Buddhism and zen that they practice in Japan, and teach their children, is very close to what we have in Bible school in the black church. It's about humanism, respect, and loving people. My love for the Japanese may stem in part from the love I felt for my close Japanese friend in junior high school, Kiyoshi Mikawa.

I want to have a mixed company, but most of the white dancers who can dance at the level of my kids are off doing either television or films. At times, I've had superb white artists, such as Linda Kent, Jonathan Riseling, and Maxine Sherman. Maxine is with Martha Graham now; she left because she said she would never get to do *Cry*, and she was right. Even though she had every other leading part in the repertoire except *Cry*, she said, "I'm going back to Martha Graham." Other dancers in the company feel the same way. They're convinced that I favor the black dancers and that I'm never going to put an Asian or a Caucasian above the black women in my company. My response is they've danced the other leading parts, except for *Cry*, which is dedicated to my mother and black women everywhere.

If I didn't have to get caught up in the swirl of budgets, I could probably do even more artistically. In the early days I was careless about money (not that there was ever that much), and *Revelations* and *Blues Suite* were big productions with lots of costumes for which I didn't stint. But nowadays I think the costs through more carefully. At the present time I'm preparing a ballet from music by Jay McShann. I have a budget and wonderful costumes for sixteen people. It's going to cost $1,000 per costume, or $16,000 right there. I ask myself, Shall I have this piece of scenery or can I live without it? And that's the rough part. I like to do whatever I feel will enhance the production, but as the resident choreographer it's up to me to be creative with what we have.

The ballet about Charlie Parker, *For Bird With Love*, was

supposed to cost $90,000 but ended up costing $125,000. The major expense was for rehearsals, something like $30,000 a week. Then we had the staff, the designers, lighting and scenery, costumes to be made, and music to be edited. In the early years I had all live music; using singers came out of the musical comedy and vaudeville tradition that I first saw at the Lincoln Theater in Los Angeles as a schoolboy. It also came out of my Texas childhood, where I heard people like Blind Lemon Jefferson and itinerant singers and guitarists playing at Saturday night parties. In the early version of *Blues Suite* the dancers sang. Until we started touring, which necessitated the use of tapes, we always had live music at our concerts. Besides Brother John, I once had a wonderful lady singer named Nancy Redi.

There's a different climate today in terms of funding. Back in the 1940s and 1950s, when I started my company, there was no climate of funding at all. Katherine Dunham, for example, never saw a nickel from any federal, state, or city source. I understand there were some individuals who would give her a couple of thousand dollars every now and then, and to keep a company going for twenty years with virtually no financial help is remarkable. By the time I started out, the Dunham company had folded; there was no permanent black company, only pickup groups. The first funding came along in 1966 when the National Endowment for the Arts was formed; the following year the NEA gave me a grant of $10,000. I thought I was absolutely rich. I tried to make twelve ballets with that $10,000, and that's how the first deficit came about. I was swimming in productions. Ivy Clark, our company manager, said, "You can't do this, Alvin. You don't have that much money."

And money, no matter how successful you are, no matter how critically acclaimed, is a problem that never entirely goes away. It's always up and down. You go through five years when your books are good, money is being raised, you're touring, and then *bam*—you're back to square one. An example is the Dunham project, which is part of our effort to preserve and present the work of other great choreographers. We're almost $200,000 over budget; we have a $400,000 deficit and rehearsals coming up in July for which there is no money.

The financial folks try to keep these kinds of things away from me, though I always know generally where we are. Not until it gets rather grim do they come to me. I attend board meetings; I meet with groups of people; I do fund-raising myself by going to lunches and galas and making speeches here and there. In this business, life is one long fund-raising effort.

Of course, it is known that in the funding community there are two dance worlds and two very different ways of thinking. There is, first of all, the ballet world, which gets the lion's share of the money. Their budgets are bigger. They need pointe shoes, they need pianists. Then there's the modern dance world, which is barefoot and not elitist. Automatically, because of its elite position in everybody's mind, having come, as it did, from the royal courts over the centuries, classical ballet is the funding world's pet project.

Young people today also have a different attitude about money from when I started out. They are more concerned with how much they can make. Sometimes I wonder whether, in today's climate, I would be encouraged to be a choreographer— whether it would be as easy an entrée as it was in 1958. Despite all the change, though, it's still a worthwhile thing to me to work in the dance world. I still love it, and I'm very enthusiastic about the young people we develop.

After thirty years as head of the company, I've given a lot of thought to a successor. There are several candidates. My choice would be Gary DeLoatch, who I think could lead the company in new and exciting directions. I believe the board, though, would prefer somebody like Judy Jamison because of fund-raising possibilities that are inherent in her. Time will tell.

You have to accept that the day will come when you physically can't do it anymore. When I'm making a ballet, my life is very intense, but I do that only once or twice a year, so it really isn't that big a strain on me—not yet, anyway. Still, I wouldn't mind seeing another artistic director come on board. I want to go to Paris for one or two years. I want to go to Tahiti, I want to go to the Bahamas, I want to go to Africa. I can't fulfill all those dreams when I'm still so attached to the company.

Because of the way things have evolved over the past thirty years, I am pretty much free now. I have a wonderful associate artistic director, Mary Barnett, who knows exactly what I think—we're like one. And other people underneath her, ballet masters, can run things. As a matter of fact, the whole enterprise can run without me; I don't have to be there all the time. It allows me the freedom to go away and choreograph when there are no rehearsals at home. Indeed, I went away for two months in February and March to La Scala and made pieces there. I do look forward to the day when I can be even more distant.

TWELVE

Going, Going, Gone
(Almost)

What I remember most vividly was the sound of ambulances, the sounds of New York City. The ambulance was taking me away into the whirling sounds of silence. I was strapped into a city ambulance with two medical attendants, one on either side, my mother holding my hand. We were ripping through the city at seven o'clock in the morning. Everybody else was going to work, and I was going God knows where.

I remember the music of the sirens, the horror in my head, as we passed from Manhattan into Queens and then Westchester. We finally arrived someplace with me still strapped down, still holding my mother's hand, still with those two people looking down at me. My mind was confused and fraught with dread. I remember signing a lot of papers and saying goodbye to my mother. I was inside a little room with a woman sitting outside the door. I didn't have the slightest idea where the hell I was.

After a while, they let me go outside to pee. I was in a place with a long corridor that people were wandering through. I asked a woman, "Where am I?" She said, "You're in a mental institution." A mental institution, I soon learned, was full of people with a lot of disturbances, full of doctors, full of agony. It was a velvet cage, a place to be guarded, a place to be kept from the public, a place I had been moving toward for the last several months. I was very upset about this, but I knew that I deserved all that was happening to me.

For several months before that morning I had been the most incredible manic-depressive person that one could imagine. It had started in October 1979; I was sitting on a bed with a glass of brandy, and somebody came into my room in Luxembourg, where we were on tour with the company. He told me that my good friend Joyce Trisler had died. "How's that possible?" I asked. Joyce and I had gone back all the way to the Lester Horton days. Joyce with the scrawny legs; Joyce with the gentle humor. We became really close friends when I came to New York. She was an intelligent girl who knew a lot of things I didn't know. She had a fantastic sensibility as a dancer and a very interesting, long, loose body. Lester used to call her a rag doll because she was so loose. She was a crazy girl and very funny. Joyce wasn't poor like the rest of us. Carmen de Lavallade, Jimmy Truitte, and I were from the ghetto and were suffering from being black in Los Angeles. Joyce was an upper-middle-class girl who didn't need anything but was giving herself completely to the idea of what Lester was doing. He created several ballets on her while I was around.

Her death shocked me. It was totally unexpected. Joyce had been drinking; everybody could see that. She was very thin, very wild, and full of rage. She would say, "Those motherfuckers can't tell me what to do. I'm writing a proposal. The New York State Council on the Arts and the National Endowment on the Arts better take it. I'll show them my reviews. They should give me the money to keep my company together." I probably have that same kind of rage about those funding agencies, but I had never let it out.

Joyce started to drink, and everybody talked about her. She would come to school a little tipsy. I was very concerned and had several talks with her about her drinking. I remember we went to a bar where she drank a lot of scotch. I said, "Joyce, do you really want to drink that much?" "Don't tell me what to do," she said. "If I like scotch, I like scotch." It turned out that Joyce had died from drinking scotch late one night combined with some Valium and a couple of sleeping pills. I think her death was probably an accident. Joyce was not the kind of personality to kill herself. She was a very giving, humorous person who conducted her classes with humor. We have seeds of the Horton technique at the Ailey School today, seeds planted by her and Jimmy Truitte.

Joyce's death took me to a place in my mind that I never thought I would visit or even knew existed. I have never been the same since her death. She was forty-eight; Lester Horton was forty-seven when he died. I immediately thought, Well, if Joyce can die, you can die. I was afraid I would die immediately. So in October 1979 I decided to live quickly and get all that I could from what time I had left. The company moved on to Paris, and I connected with Abdullah, an Arab boy whom I had met earlier in Paris. We found the best hashish and the best cognac in town and began to smoke and drink like two wild people—and to enjoy each other. After completing our season in Paris, I went back to New York, still holding within me the agony of Joyce's death.

I had seen Joyce just before leaving home for our European tour. We had talked about dance companies; we had talked about love; we had talked about passion; we had talked about what we were trying to do with our lives, about how important it was to make beautiful dance. After returning from the tour I had to go immediately to the opening of our school in the Minskoff Building on West Forty-fifth Street. Joyce had always been a part of the school. I got off the plane at two o'clock in the afternoon and had just enough time to run upstairs, comb my hair, snort a little cocaine, and run downstairs to one of the studios to make a speech. I remember saying, "This school belongs to everybody. This is going to be a place where we can make dances, where we can learn to love each other as human beings, where we can keep the techniques alive." I never mentioned Joyce.

To me it was still incredible that she should actually have died; there had been so much life in her, even with all her problems. In some deep part of me I guess I simply refused to accept it. I didn't cry, I didn't feel depressed; I locked the truth of her death away inside my heart. It became like a locked door to me, a door I wouldn't open until after the session in the mental hospital when I went to see *Memoria* at the City Center. I left the theater in tears. Making the dance had been a deep experience for me, and some say it's one of my best works. I was high all the time I created it.

It was early November, shortly after Joyce's death, when I started working on *Memoria*. As usual, when I went into rehearsal, I didn't know what I was doing at the beginning. I tried many different kinds of music, some Bach, some Ellington, and started working on this dance without a center, without a focus. Finally I called Donna Wood to rehearse the role of a woman wandering in space, and after about three weeks of work on the dance I began to realize that it was about Joyce. I also did something I had never done before, which was to include the second company and all the workshop students in the ballet. Everybody thought I was crazy. Which I was—cocaine crazy. I had a little vial, and every time there was a break, I'd do some cocaine, looking for that rush, that up. *Memoria* is a broader piece than I would have done without having the cocaine. It was the cocaine high that made me think big and put all these people in the second part called *A Season of Hell*.

Memoria had wonderfully evocative music by Keith Jarrett. *Memoria* is about Joyce's life, my memories of her, my image of her. Although these are very abstract images, nobody has ever asked me what *Memoria* is about. People everywhere understand it. Making the dance was a very deep and wrenching experience for me.

It's interesting how my personal relationships affect my creativity. It seems as though nearly all of my dances have some basis in an event or a feeling I've had that I can usually trace. I'm now working on a dance that has to do with the image of a black woman, a ghost who dies and comes back to her man. It's an idea, based on a famous New Orleans story, that's been floating around in my head for a long time. I think it's going to be a ballet for Judy's company.

During this period I kept having extreme mood swings— with more ups than downs. I wouldn't allow myself to get really down. When the manic phase and my mind would whirl like a hurricane, I would do and say and feel extraordinary things. Shortly before Joyce's death, in 1979, a longtime friend had suggested that maybe a little hit of cocaine would help me solve my problems and reduce my sense of despair. Around that time I met a wonderful man, a steady cocaine user who lived not far from me. Before long I was spending three to four hundred dollars a week on the drug. I used it for everything. I put it in champagne, in Perrier water. My whole life became centered on cocaine and sundry drugs. I had a little box in which there was Valium and an assortment of other mind-altering powders. I took cocaine day and night. Under its influence I decided that I was free to do whatever I wanted to do. I would not allow myself to be like Lester and just submit to death. I would not be like Joyce, who slipped away in the middle of the night. I would live my life to the very fullest.

I started spending money lavishly—a destructive side effect that's associated with this particular mental illness. I decided that in order to travel properly a man of my stature needed to have a limousine, so I had a limousine company on call at all times. I went on shopping sprees, smoking pot and snorting cocaine as I bought clothes and jewelry and anything else that caught my fancy. I bought whatever I felt like buying—the hell with the price—and threw it in the back of the limousine.

Miguel Algarín is owner-director of the Nuyorican Poets Cafe—a big loftlike space on the Lower East Side with a twenty- to twenty-five-foot ceiling. There's a balcony with an orange stairway that leads up to it. One night I decided it would be gorgeous to have candles lighting this space, little candles in glass. So I went next door and spent a lot of money on candles— Miguel recalls (I do not) that I bought every candle the store had. I took these candles, lit them, and very slowly, in front of the audience dancing down below, walked up the thirty steps, leaving a lit candle on each one. I also put candles along the edges of the balcony and the trestles. When the lights were turned off, the place was like Lourdes. I was high—totally stoned while doing this.

In another room at the cafe I would produce cocaine purchased from my man, my Sporting Life, spread it on a table, and invite special friends to feast on my white powder. It was a very bad period. A very, very bad period.

Playwright Miguel Piñero, who wrote *Short Eyes,* and I did some extraordinary things. You have to imagine me being driven downtown in a long black limousine, late-thirties vintage, with an open top. Miguel and I would often drive through the Lower East Side, standing on the backseat of the limo, with our heads and bodies out, waving to the people in the street. They would yell, "Hey, it's Mikey. Hey, Mikey!" They didn't know who I was. We were waving like the pope, both of us totally spaced out of our minds.

I also fixed the cafe's lighting booth. The machine was broken, and no one knew how to repair it. I had learned something about lighting from working with Lester Horton. I arranged the lights so they would flash, disco style. The young kids, the seventeen- and eighteen-year-olds, were fascinated by that and would ask me to show them how to work the lighting booth. That's how I got to be King of the Cafe.

One night Miguel Piñero's sister sat in a corner of the cafe looking at me very strangely. She then turned her face to the wall. Miguel huddled with her, talking in whispers, and then said to me, "My sister says you have a *caldo negro,* a warm black something over your face. Something is not happening right with you. You are not well. You have to be careful." This was the immediate impression I made on a woman I had just met.

Miguel and I often stayed at the cafe until three o'clock in the morning. If I didn't come in a limousine, he or another friend would drive me home to 107th Street. Often, Miguel and I would get pot and cocaine and continue partying up at my place.

The cocaine took me on some extraordinary adventures— many now blurred in my mind and a few of them far from safe. I had a big police dog I adored named Lucky, and sometimes when I was riding a high I would take Lucky and go running in Central Park for hours. I'm sure poor Lucky was exhausted. At other times I would go to the neighborhood supermarket, where I felt that everything belonged to me, and I would take whatever I wanted home with me without bothering to pay. Someone from the supermarket would come and get me. I couldn't understand why I was being treated like a common thief. This sometimes resulted in street scuffles, and more than once I ended up in the hospital. The police in the neighborhood knew me well; I didn't understand why they knew me, being too far gone to connect it to my stealing.

In December 1979, I had brought Abdullah from Paris to New York. This, I vowed, was going to be the perfect relationship. In my craziness I introduced this very innocent twenty-two-year-old to cocaine, to marijuana, to a variety of exotic drugs. I also introduced him to the Lower East Side and to the magic of dentistry. I bought him suits and shirts and ties and shoes, all of which he looked terrific in. He was very attractive, and people would go after him on the streets. He did the normal straight-boy things: He had a girlfriend, a blonde from Long Island, whom he would spend a lot of time with, and this drove me crazy with jealousy. But he would always come back.

Finally, in the middle of one of my parties with Miguel and several young Puerto Ricans of dubious reputation, Abdullah went down the fire escape and left. I never saw him again. I've gone over it so many times in my mind from every angle, and I've come to the conclusion that my lifestyle was destroying him. He couldn't approve of, or accept, the values I lived by day after day. He couldn't believe, for example, that I would pay somebody seventy-five dollars for an ounce of pot. He was aghast.

My crazy mind told me he was at the International House, where, searching for a relationship with people of his own kind, he had made friends with some Moroccan. So I went over there, at the very height of the manic state I was in. Like a madman I raced up and down the dormitory rooms knocking on doors. I then went back to the main desk and demanded that they produce Abdullah. They said there was nobody there by that name, nobody who fit the description I gave them. I got furious and kicked a table in their office and a couple of other loose objects.

First the campus police arrived, followed shortly by the city police. They handcuffed me. I was screaming obscenities as they bundled me into a car and rushed me to Bellevue and sedated me. I was locked up in a straitjacket. Everybody I knew came to see me, which was the last thing I wanted.

After eight days, I was let out of Bellevue. And in my mind I said goodbye to Abdullah, and that really upset me terribly because I felt responsible for him, and I also felt the full force of his rejection. He took with him some silver and coins that I had collected. He had obviously planned to leave, and planned to leave with something of mine, which goes to the part of my life that's involved with young men who take things. I seem to be drawn to such young men, believing each time that it will not happen—that they will stay, that they will be above theft. However, because I knew Abdullah and was all too aware of the reasons why he left, I refuse to put him in the category of young men who take things.

Nineteen eighty was a bad year. I did erratic and unforgivable things—firing six people from the office in one of my manic moods, calling my mother and saying ridiculous things, constantly putting the heavy burden of our friendship on my friends. I suffered from a growing paranoia. Sometimes, late at night, I would call for a limousine, feeling an overpowering urge to go somewhere. Anywhere. The car would come to a red light, which had become the symbol of fear, the symbol of paranoia, the clear signal that someone was chasing me; and to avoid facing the ghastly redness, I would lie down in the back of the limo and tell the driver where I wanted to go. He must have thought I was nuts—which I was. But he would take me wherever I wanted to go, with me lying in the back, riven with dread.

Nineteen eighty was also a year when I spent an increasing amount of my time with those friends who were involved with dope. Doing cocaine was the chic thing to be into back then.

"Cocaine is not disruptive" was our position; we thought of it as purely recreational. There was no cocaine crisis at that time. The DEA wasn't patrolling the borders to keep cocaine out in 1980. Heroin was the scary drug; cocaine was fun. The people I did drugs with were hip people—writers, musicians, composers. We treated cocaine like a social drug. None of us thought it was addictive.

Before Joyce Trisler's death, I had never had a problem with drugs or alcohol. In fact, when I arrived in New York City in 1958, I didn't drink and didn't dream of taking drugs. Until 1965, the year I discovered marijuana, I was a very pure boy. Before that, I thought smoking weed was something that only crazy people did. The idea of hyping my creativity with anything stronger than coffee would not have occurred to me. When I thought of drugs at all, I thought they would make me into a less interesting person.

But by 1980 everything had changed. My friends and I would go to clubs where cocaine was available, and we'd smoke and snort until five, six, seven o'clock in the morning. Sometimes we'd go to the house of a woman friend who was a composer and freebase cocaine with her. If we ran out of cocaine, no problem—we'd drive to New Jersey to get more. My paranoia grew so extreme that I would sometimes walk from my apartment on 107th Street and Central Park West down to my office on Forty-fifth Street disguised in a black ski cap and carrying an umbrella. The thing that finally got me into the hospital, in May, was my decision that in order to attract more attention I should discreetly start a fire. Gripped by this insanity, I ran up and down the hallways of seventeen floors, knocking on everybody's doors at 11 P.M. screaming, *"Fire! Fire!"* When the police and fire trucks came, I was sitting across the street on a park bench watching them from a distance.

A few days later I told a white lady in my building that I

wanted to see the inside of her apartment. Lucky, my German shepherd, was with me. I pushed my way in and looked around. It was an impressive place, tastefully furnished, and I decided that it all belonged to me. When I walked out of her apartment, I left Lucky there. Soon I was once again running through the building screaming, *"Fire! Fire! Fire!"* Another lady from the building came outside and saw me sitting calmly on the bench across the street. She told the police that I was the guy screaming fire and that I'd done it before. When the police came over to question me, one recognized me from previous encounters. I was then taken to the hospital, where I was loaded up with tranquilizers.

The lady whose apartment I had invaded against her will pressed charges, and I was booked for assault. (It wasn't assault, but I had scared the shit out of her.) I was put in the pen with everybody else. About seven the next morning I was brought out front, where my mother and my lawyer were waiting. My mother said I had the choice of going to jail or to the hospital. I said, "I'll go to the hospital."

The hospital, Bloomingdale Center, set among trees on a hill in Westchester County, was like an ancient Tudor castle. In that elegant setting I was told that I was a manic-depressive, a diagnosis that scared me to death. "How *dare* you tell me I'm manic-depressive," I shouted. "I'll sue you for that." But the symptoms of manic-depressive disorder certainly sounded familiar to me. Part of the manic-depressive trip is two-sided: On the downswing you're in darkness where you feel like you're just nobody, you're nothing—a state that fit right into my chronic sense of inferiority. On the upswing you're king—you're on top of the world. You're the man with the limousine. Everybody needs you and wants you. Then, on top of all the rest, there's the paranoia which often rages out of control.

I spent seven weeks in Bloomingdale Center, in a small

room. It was a decent place with very good food and a well-equipped gymnasium. I soon got into peak physical shape. They also had crafts, and I made boxes. There were interesting people there. My best friend was a young guy in his late twenties named Mark. He was there because one night he had found himself on the roof of his house in Long Island, naked.

During my stay at the hospital a number of neurological tests and urological examinations were done on me. I was given large doses of medication, and there were many sessions with the psychiatrist—group therapy, one-to-one therapy. But there was no mention of drugs. I never told the staff or anyone in group or individual therapy that I had been on drugs, and no one ever asked. We never discussed drugs. It was only after I got back home and saw my drug box with all the stuff still in it that I said, "You asshole, you never told those people you were on drugs. That would have solved it all." To me, my manic-depression was triggered by drug usage, especially cocaine. I hadn't touched cocaine until 1979, when Joyce died. It had all started with the hashish and brandy with Abdullah in Paris, had started with the belief that I had to do something with myself because I might die at any moment. That if I didn't live quickly, if I didn't do whatever I had to do, didn't live out my fantasies, it would be too late. I eventually reached the point where I had cocaine for breakfast and was spending four or five hundred dollars a week on it and on other drugs.

My cocaine trip lasted from October 1979 until July 1980, when I entered the hospital. The hospital finally released me when they discovered that lithium worked, that it cleared my head and made me normal. About two weeks before I left they said, "We think you're going to be able to go home." That was great because, at first, given the apparent severity of my case, they had thought I was going to be forced to spend the rest of my life in a mental hospital.

When I was released, I had no place to go. My mother came up to New York when she learned that I was being discharged. The fact that she and my brother had been there when I was taken to the hospital really meant a lot. My mother is a very, very sensitive woman. She felt from talking to me on the phone before I was hospitalized, when I said ridiculous, irrational things, that something was very, very wrong. She and I drove to a hotel on Madison Avenue and Seventy-seventh Street, and she stayed there with me for three weeks, seeing that I was all right, cooking, being motherly. I stayed on another week by myself and then moved to the Chelsea Hotel, where I spent another month while looking for a place to live.

That posthospital period was very traumatic. When I got out, I was upset and frightened because there had been a lot of publicity in the papers. I was afraid after reading about my running up and down the stairway doing all this manic stuff, no owner of an apartment building would take me as a tenant. I was also upset that people would recognize me on the streets. My picture had been plastered all over the newspapers. It took me a long time before I would go out in public and face people. Going back to the school, for example, after all that had happened, was one of the hardest things I ever did. My mother said, "Alvin, you've got to go over there, you know, sooner or later." So one day I got all dressed up and presented myself at the offices of the school. I was afraid that somebody would say, "He's a crazy number." Instead, they all made my return as easy as possible, considering the circumstances.

Some wonderful people came to my aid. The theater critic Clive Barnes, for example, called me after I got out of the hospital. He said that who I was, the pieces I had done, my company and my accomplishments, were certainly bigger than the problems I was going through. That helped a lot. I am an insecure man, a man who wonders who he is, a man from small-town

Texas who never forgot walking through dirt with his mother as a child looking for a place to live. It's part of a great insecurity that I've always lived with. Zita Allen wrote an article in the *Village Voice* which said that "Alvin Ailey may be paying dues for fifty years of agony." My illness, I now understand, was the way that agony manifested itself. I never understood or faced that truth, not for many years. My way has always been to take things at face value, for what they are. The agony of being black, the agony of coming from small-town Texas and ending up dancing on the Champs Elysées in Paris, was a heavy load to carry. The contrast, the cultural distance between those two points, certainly had something to do with my illness.

If I go awhile without taking the lithium, I find myself occasionally slipping back into depression. The depression is the part that says, Why am I doing this? Why do I want a dance company? I'm tired of the whole goddamned thing. I'm tired of begging people for money.

One thing I learned from the experience of mentally melting down was how to delegate responsibility. I was under the impression that I could and should do everything, cross every *t* dot every *i*. I was involved not only with the AAADT, but with the second company, the Alvin Ailey Repertory Ensemble, the school, the board, everything. I learned that I could not do all that, learned that responsibility had to be delegated, that I had to trust people.

My first ballet out of the hospital was a tough one. I was very fearful about *Phases*. I wondered if I could make a ballet anymore. How much of the craziness was a part of what I was as a creative person? I had the music by Max Roach around the house for a long time. And it worked. Which tells me a lot, tells me that I can go on.

I was suddenly very happy. Rationally happy, the best kind of happiness you can have.

Remembrances of Alvin

$\mathcal{S}$ometime in mid-November 1989, I received a phone call from Alvin Ailey's mother, Mrs. Lula Cooper. We had met for the first time in January 1989 when she was in New York City to visit Alvin while he was in the hospital. He called and asked me to come to the city to meet and interview his mother.

I arrived the next day from Virginia, and over the next two days I spent several hours with Alvin, his mother, his brother, Calvin Cooper, and a dozen other friends who visited while I was there. When Alvin wasn't sleeping, greeting his visitors, or dealing with his nurse, we talked very generally about several things, including our progress on his autobiography. He named additional people he wanted me to interview.

I still smile when I think of one incident that occurred during my visits. Mrs. Cooper, Calvin, Alvin, and I were seated around his bed. Suddenly, and very dramatically, he asked them to leave the room briefly, "because Peter and I have to talk."

Once they left, Alvin asked me in a clear and firm voice, "You got any pot?" I was surprised at his request, because although Alvin and I had known each other for nearly twenty years, we did not have a social relationship involving more than my occasionally joining him for a drink in one of his favorite watering holes, usually after an interview session. "I need a stimulant," he said. I told him I didn't have any pot and that even if I did, he couldn't light up in his room without blowing the place up with all that equipment around. "What about some brandy or beer," he persisted. "You can sneak it into the room." "Not me," I said, "I'm too chicken to try stuff like that." Reluctantly he dropped the idea.

There was so much activity in his room that there was no opportunity for taping. When I returned to Richmond, I left the tape recorder with Mrs. Cooper in case Alvin wanted to say anything before I flew back to New York the following weekend. The opportunity never presented itself. A day or so after my visit, Alvin went into swift physical deterioration. The difference between the Alvin I left that Sunday evening and the Alvin I saw when I returned on Saturday was disturbing and profound. The Alvin I left a week earlier, though at times forgetful, was talking, smiling, and greeting visitors. The Alvin I saw upon my return was no longer talking or recognizing anyone. I left the hospital after several hours, convinced that the end was near. Two or three days later, on December 1, 1989, I got the call saying he had died of a rare blood disease.

Besides family members and friends, Alvin was survived by the Dance Theater Foundation, Inc., a not-for-profit organization that administers the AAADT; the Alvin Ailey American Dance Center, an accredited academy of dance education which currently serves some three thousand students each year; and the Alvin Ailey Repertory Ensemble, the junior resident company of the school. Students in the school come from all over the world.

Alvin's death came five days before AAADT's 1989 season

opened at the City Center. Immediate plans were made to feature opening night as an all-Ailey evening. A full house of Ailey devotees turned out for what became an emotional event, a mixture of sadness about his death and joy about his life and his creativity. Company members, dancing with genuine love and emotion, showed once again why Alvin was a giant in the field of modern dance. By the time the long evening closed with a celebratory version of *Revelations,* there were tears in the eyes of most of the audience, but there was also the joy of seeing brilliant choreography danced brilliantly by the AAADT. It was very clear that Alvin will live through the performing of his ballets.

Much of this was repeated a short time later at a memorial service for Alvin held at New York City's Cathedral of St. John the Divine. "When a giant tree falls, the forest trembles," said poet and former dancer Maya Angelou. Two of Alvin's "dancing divas," Carmen de Lavallade and Judith Jamison, gave moving tributes to an artist who had created beautiful ballets for both of them. Donna Wood danced the shout segment from *Cry;* Dudley Williams danced the "I Want to Be Ready" segment from *Revelations;* John Parks and Mari Kajiwara danced the "Fix Me, Jesus" segment from *Revelations,* while company members did the exciting "Rocka My Soul" segment from the same ballet. As with the opening-night tribute, it was an occasion for celebrating the creative contributions and genius of a world-class choreographer who had sometimes caused trouble for himself and others, who had sometimes been " 'buked and scorned," but who knew how to rock souls.

During the last three or four months of Alvin's life, I knew he was sick. Our time together became precious; every minute we had to talk added another anecdote, a suddenly recalled fragment of his life, to what you're reading here. Alvin had reached a pinnacle in the New York City, national, and international art worlds that enabled him to see and experience much that is denied to most black artists. He was aware that this world, while accepting him, believes that European music and dance are vastly superior to all other music and dance. In his mind and heart he knew this to be an arrogant lie, but he deeply craved acceptance and recognition from those who promoted such views. This ambivalence came through rather frequently in our conversations. Sometimes he would complain about what he perceived as a slight from one of the perpetrators of the myth, and I wanted to say, "Alvin, don't you know who you are? Set that person straight." But he didn't have the heart to fight the white establishment.

Alvin responded to his illness by directing me to interview people he had not been in contact with for years. Some of these people had been hurt deeply by him, but I sensed that he wanted me to get down on paper a full and honest portrait of his life—wrinkles and all.

He especially wanted me to speak with Ivy Clark, from whom he had been long estranged. Her firing by the AAADT in 1975 had been a major topic of conversation in the black dance world. Though their relationship was irrevocably shattered, Alvin, in the Twentieth Anniversary Program, written and edited by Zita Allen, said, "Ivy Clark spent seven years dragging the company up by its bootstraps. From 1968 to 1975, Ivy was the very soul of this company. I mean she was the right hand, my left leg, everything. She came on in 1968 as a wardrobe mistress when everything was just a mess. I had just taken our first National Endowment for the Arts grant of $10,000 and, thinking I was rich, tried to make ten ballets with it. Ivy was the one who apprised me of the fact that we are losing money, spending more than we made and that we now had to up our fee in order to pay our expenses. She took everything in hand, turning it around, and gave us a big push in the right direction. She was just phenomenal. Without Ivy Clark's divine determination and love there would be no Ailey company today."

I followed Alvin's instructions and spoke to the people whose names I had been given. Some of the interviews were conducted before his death, others a month to four months afterward. Here they are, those who loved Alvin as well as those who learned from him and respected his art, remembering him in their own words.

A. Peter Bailey

Miguel Algarín, professor of English literature, Rutgers University; director of Nuyorican Poets Cafe

When Alvin came to the cafe he was like a shaman, a crazy man, crazy in terms of the energy he released in the room. We had two light boards which he would work furiously, driving the energy in the room into a frenzy while people were dancing. He didn't sit still at any point. He had to constantly go, go, go.

I once had no ending to a play I was doing, so I told my sound man I was going to open the door and let Alvin in. I knew he was going to come in like God and start ordering people to stop doing this, start doing that. When he came in, I told the cast to follow him. In a mad flurry of five minutes he created this movement for the company that closed the play. Alvin never saw the play because he was put away shortly afterward.

Clarence Barnett, friend and confidant

Alvin told me that he wanted Carmen to run his company, but first he had to apologize to Geoffrey Holder, her husband, for once treating Carmen insensitively. Geoffrey wouldn't accept his apology and told him to go away. He wanted Carmen because she was a smart, well-educated, very sophisticated, strong woman. After he died, they would never take her because she had too much sense.

Charles Blackwell, stage manager for early concerts

Alvin, the dancer, was fantastic. First of all was the excitement of seeing a linebacker dance. He looked like Herschel Walker looks now, except he had grace. Walker has a kind of power and grace, but Alvin was just a gorgeous dancer. He also had a big heart, and all of this was on the stage. This was exciting because there were many dance companies where that wasn't on the stage. I loved it because he was doing stuff that had not been done that way before. As a stage manager I loved his theatricality. He told us that he didn't want his concerts done the traditional way, where you dance, the curtain comes down, they have bows, and then you wait ten minutes while things are changed. Then you go on to the next dance. He wanted it run like a musical, which we did. We made the show flow. In *Revelations,* things went from beginning to end, so you could see his choreography. You could see the thrust of his drama because there wasn't technical jargon getting in the way.

The highlight I remember from the second concert occurred after the performance. When you're a big man, the size of your body prevents you from being considered vulnerable. Everybody depends on your strength. They ask you for help, you have no one to ask. That was Alvin, doing all this work, holding on, being steadfast and focused. When the curtain came down on that stage, Alvin sat down and cried. Everything he had held in for everybody else's sake came out. It was memorable.

Ivy Clark, former company general manager

Artistically and theatrically, Alvin was fantastic. He knew exactly what would work and how it would work. He would just look and know how to position people, how to get them on and offstage. He was musical. He had a color sense, he had a music sense, and he had excellent taste for the finer things in life. I'm sorry that this interview is taking place after his death. I wish he had been alive when you came to me because there are so many things that we could discuss back and forth, he and I, the three of us.

George Faison, former AAADT dancer and award-winning choreographer

I was a student at Howard University when I first saw the Alvin Ailey American Dance Theater. When the curtains opened, my life flowed out from the wings. I had never seen anything like that in my life, the energy, the bearing. I thought, "That's what I want to be." We saw the most impeccable human beings, the most flawless bodies I had ever seen, dancing to rhythms that had only been in my head. Morton Winston was absolutely incredible. That was the male dancer I wanted to be. He danced with a kind of arrogance which I liked. There was also Jimmy Truitte, Dudley Williams, Miguel Godreau, Loretta Abbott. It was like when you come upon your first sunset or sunrise. I was gone. I said, "Oh God, that's what I have to do."

Alvin was intelligent, but he was naive in a certain way about how people really love each other, how people ultimately talk to each other. He learned it gradually over his life, and we had a real friendship toward the end, but there was still this coldness. Our problem was that Alvin had a lot of people around him who believed that if it's black, whether choreography or music, it's mediocre. Once, in regard to my piece *Suite Otis,* he said, "George when are you going to choreograph a ballet with real music?" I said, "What are you talking about? Are you saying that Otis Redding's music is not real music?" He seemed to have stopped believing that his culture possessed all the things that he was searching for in somebody else's culture.

When we begin to think of Alvin in a historical context, we must always remember that there has always been a debate about the artistic accomplishment of black choreographers and black dancers. They've been viewed as existing outside of mainstream modern dance. We discovered this when we began to develop an American Dance Festival program. We were interested in doing a script for a possible documentary. In the process of pulling our facts together, we discovered not only white dancers but black dancers who did not know the scope of African-American participation in the history of dance.

When you look at Alvin's company souvenir booklet and see the repertoire from 1958 to 1989 it's astounding. It's the most extraordinary repertoire in the whole history of modern dance. There's something for everyone. Alvin wanted his dancers to be dancing actors and actresses, and that's how Alvin did his works. He made us feel ourselves in the dance. This is why audiences around the world responded to Alvin Ailey. It's referred to as empathic kinetics. It sounds technical, but basically it causes an audience to clap, tap their feet, or move with the dancers onstage. And this is what happens to you when you attend a performance of Alvin's company.

Ellis Haizlip, friend and AAADT board member

I saw the first concert in 1958 and found it absolutely brilliant. Alvin was one of the most physically gorgeous people that has ever been onstage. My personal favorite of his ballets is *Revelations*. It has that spiritual base, and it's beautiful beyond belief. I think it's one of the few dance masterpieces in the world. There's a rich legacy in black culture, and Alvin wasn't afraid to preserve it as he perceived it. *Night Creatures, Blues Suite*—all these kinds of pieces represented real people.

His company grew to the point where the organization was beyond his own personal management. He and Ivy were forced to recognize that Alvin had to take on a board of directors in order to move into significant funding. He had some problems with the board because he wished he had money to pour into his work. The board very rarely questioned Alvin's artistic integrity and supported him to the extent that it could with funding. But he had a problem with it. Alvin didn't necessarily hang out with his board members. He had this personal persona that was very private. I don't remember his ever having the board into his apartment for dinner or drinks or anything like that. He needed to be more outgoing to those people who helped him, needed to relate to them in a closer manner. He just wasn't close to them in that way, but he was close to them in whatever the company was doing publicly.

Nat Horne, former dancer with the AAADT

Alvin was very good at working with a dancer's natural ability. He would often see things and take from us what he saw. He wanted technique, but if you didn't have a lot of technique, he built off what you had. He was good at using natural feelings. That's why *Revelations* works so well. Dancing is expressing emotions, and he used them so well. *Revelations,* a spiritual piece, and *Blues Suite* have roots in the basic blues feelings of black people. Thus they both have good foundations, and when you build something on a strong foundation, it just doesn't fall down. It can only go so low even on its worst day. And on their worst days, they were super. Alvin was successful because his company was built on the foundation of a group of people who. believed in him and who believed in what they were doing. Minnie Marshall, Herman Howell, Charles Moore, Ella Thompson, Lavinia Hamilton—they were all wonderful.

Judith Jamison

In 1963, I was a student at the Philadelphia Dance Academy. We were assigned to go and see the Alvin Ailey American Dance Theater perform in a small theater. I had seen a few pictures of the company in books, but that was it. It was there I saw *Revelations* for the first time. Alvin was doing "Wading in the Water." He weighed about three hundred pounds at the time, but it didn't make a bit of difference. He moved like a cat, with just an extraordinary quality of movement that I had never seen before. That's my criterion when I look for dancers now, that they move distinctly differently from each other. Alvin did. His hands were like liquid. His body rippled. He had a marvelous presence, an energy and a dynamic that were unusual.

Joe Nash, black dance historian

Alvin was born in 1931, the very year that blacks for the first time entered into modern dance. How extraordinary. Katherine Dunham was in Chicago, Hemsley Winfield was in New York. It was also near the time that Farel Banga, a black performer very few people knew about, was dancing in France at the Folies. Richard Barthe has immortalized him in sculpture. It is significant that Alvin would be born at that time because prior to 1931 African Americans were primarily viewed as entertainers with superlative skills. As entertainers, they were not supposed to have a philosophy; they were not supposed to have any idea of the true significance of dance. American audiences had forgotten that blacks came from a culture where dance, the arts, music, were vital to existence. The idea of blacks as entertainers was so supreme that people just refused to accept blacks as having a desire to go into concert work. Hemsley had doors slammed in his face. The establishment refused to take him seriously. There was no interest in black culture, even from some of my own people in Harlem. In 1925, Howard University students rebelled against the use of spirituals on the campus. Yet spirituals became the foundation for black concert artists.

Alvin, being an African American in the truest sense, subscribed to the African concept of motion. Dance is emotion, action and motion. A dance is emotion in action. Consequently, all of his ballets celebrated the body moving through space in a variety of styles and techniques. Alvin celebrates the art of dance, the art of movement through space, the articulation of the body part, the total involvement of the dance in movement. Even though you see a piece that may not have the dramatic substance of earlier pieces, you still sit on the edge of your seat because of the extraordinary beauty of his dances, the excitement that they generate. People will go to an Ailey performance who don't go to see any other modern dance performance. Why? Because he lifts you up. From the very beginning Alvin always said, "I wanted to make dance available to everybody. I wanted people to be happy when they attended my performance. I wanted dances to really mean something to everybody."

When I saw *Blues Suite*, it was almost as if you were peeking in on the lives of people. And *Revelations*, oh, that opening sequence! I feel it is without a doubt the most memorable opening sequence in all of modern dance. Then there's *Cry*. It's so electric, so dynamic. I can see those three over and over again. When people question me about what is black dance or what is black tradition, I say, "We're not going to discuss it until after you see the Ailey repertoire. Then let's sit down and talk."

Harold Pierson, former AAADT dancer

My initial meeting with Alvin was when he and Carmen de Lavallade came to New York City to be featured dancers in *House of Flowers*. I had heard a little about them because they were featured dancers with Lester Horton. So the East Coast dancers were looking on with great interest. Let's be honest about it, there was a lot of resentment. It was thought and said, How dare they? What did West Coast dancers have to offer East

Coast dancers when it was a given that technically we were supposed to be the stronger of the two? I don't know if Alvin and Carmen were aware of the resentment. What Alvin and Carmen lacked on the technical end, they more than compensated for with their presence, style, and beauty.

Ernie Parham, former roommate, coproducer of the first concert

Alvin and I shared an apartment in the early years. One thing I give him a lot of credit for is that he persisted. It was very difficult back then. There were few jobs for black dancers. We really had to scuffle. I guess maybe he had a single-minded purpose. There weren't many opportunities, so he decided to make his own. He stayed here and stuck to his guns, which proves to me that if you really do work hard and don't give up and if you've got the talent, something will happen against all the odds.

Stanley Plesent, Esq., chairman of AAADT's board

Nothing was bland with Alvin. He was a man of great passion. There were times when he went through tough times. Often it would have to do with having to make changes. When he came to the decision that he had to let Ivy Clark go, that was a traumatic time for Alvin. It affected him tremendously. It was a very difficult time during which the board had to be the heavy, if you will, trying to protect Alvin against his own decision. In the last couple of years, as Alvin was becoming more and more ill, he often said, "Let's close up the company." The board existed for Alvin; he was the man. But by the time he became ill, he had created this institution with one hundred or so people depending on it for their livelihood. So when Alvin said, "Let's close down the company. I've had it. Let's do one more season and that's it," the board was put in a difficult position. What's going to happen to those dancers? What's going to happen to all those people whose beautiful creative life was part of this Ailey family? Now I don't think he ever really meant it. I think he was angry with himself because he was ill. I don't want to play the part of his therapist, but I do believe he was angry with himself because he hadn't had a good work for a couple of years. All creative people come to a point where they think their juices have dried up.

We knew that Alvin was ill for some period of time. I don't think there's any secret about that. As a board we could not ever let Alvin think that we were planning beyond him. We couldn't do that simply on the human level. On the other side, he had an obligation to all those dancers, to the teachers at the school and everybody else, to plan for the possibility that he might not be with us. So much was done quietly to prepare for that terrible eventuality. As it happened, the transition from Alvin to Judy was done with great integrity and fairness.

Brother John Sellers, artistic collaborator and friend

Alvin was a genius. I watch the younger generation of performers every now and then, but none has his charisma. They're interested in being onstage, but they aren't dedicated. Alvin was a dedicated performer. He worked hard at it. I shall never forget in Boston when he woke me up at three o'clock one morning, saying, "Brother John, we gotta rehearse." I said, "We can't rehearse. Those musicians ain't gonna get up at this time of night to rehearse." He said, "You gotta wake them up. We won't have any other time to get on the stage. Tomorrow we open." So I had to wake the musicians up. We arrived at rehearsal at four o'clock in the morning. Nobody is dedicated like that now.

I always said that Alvin had a dual personality. Sometimes he would come in and be so rotten, I'd say, "Well, the devil must have a hold on you. Your personality has changed. You have a dual personality." He'd say, "Oh, I'm just upset." But you couldn't confront the people who control the arts in New York City with that kind of attitude, especially in those days, and last. They could close so many doors in your face. Alvin had a hard time dealing with the top white people on the cultural scene. Sometimes it confused him so bad he didn't know which way to go. I used to tell him, "Alvin, you must stand still and steady yourself. You're not a church person, but I think you'd be a little better off if you went to somebody's church. We are black men. We've come up through trials and tribulations. I don't see why you are so hung up on white people all the time." He said, "Well, they can do things that others can't." I said, "I grant you that, but just don't get so hung up that you sell your own soul. Many black people deal with white people, do business with white people, but they're not as hung up as you are."

He began to get more confused when he got famous. His behavior began to get worse. He acted like he believed that he could do anything and nobody could touch him. That's the attitude he had developed. That's just the way he was. I could never get really very mad with Alvin, and he never really got mad with me. Sometimes he'd call me up at three or four o'clock in the morning and we'd talk till daybreak. This happened when he was depressed. I'd tell him, "Alvin, maybe it would help if you'd go to church." "Oh, no, no, no," he'd say.

There were fun times. Alvin could make you die laughing. We used to have fun on the road. Sometimes, when he was ready to go out, he'd say, "All right, Brother John. Tell me what the spirit says. Come on out of that house, you're too religious. Come on out of there."

Jimmy Truitte, former AAADT dancer, teacher of the
Horton technique at the school

Alvin is one of the creative geniuses of our time. But I think
that over the years he's been forced into choreography—
"You've got to come up with a new piece"—and he doesn't
work that way. Alvin has to do something when Alvin decides
he wants to do it. This is where his very, very profound works
come from. He has outlines of ballets that he has written over
the years that he wanted to do. He wants to do Henri Chris-
tophe; he wants to do Harriet Tubman. There are so many
things he wants to do, and this is what he should do—go back
and do these things. It doesn't mean that he has to go back as he
started out, solely in the black tradition, but he could do very
meaningful things. He has a steel-trap mind that is very creative.
That's why I hope he never learns to drive a car. He'd start
choreographing, take his hands off the steering wheel, and we'd
all be dead. I've always had great respect for him. But you begin
to turn out schlock if you are forced to do something before you
think you're ready. That's what people don't understand about
him. He has to do something when he's ready to.

Some evenings, when we danced, Alvin would be standing
in the wings watching. His favorite word when upset is to call
your performance "hideous." I remember one day at a rehearsal
in Yugoslavia, he went into a tirade. We had to line up on the
stage like we were in rank as he went off. Finally, I raised my
hand, stepped forward, and said, "Alvin none of us mind being
corrected if it's objective. I have never in my life given a hideous
performance. I have attained a level, and I've never sunk below
that level. Each time I try to move it up to another level. Sometimes I do that, sometimes I stay at the level I've attained, but I
never give a hideous performance." I stepped back into the line,
sure that someone else would step out and say something. I

looked down the line, but nobody moved. I said, "Oh, my God." He said, "Take ten," then, "Jimmy, come here. Do I talk too much?" he asked me. "Yes," I said, and went to the dressing room. I later asked the others why they hadn't said anything. "You said it all," they responded.

This and other things I don't hold against him. When I was forced to leave the company, the way it was handled wasn't ethical, and he knows it, but I've never held it against him, because Alvin did what he thought he had to do. If you're a friend, you take the bad with the good, and I'll always be his friend because I love him as a person and I love him as a creator.

Sylvia Waters, former AAADT dancer, company administrator

Artistically, Alvin was a many-faceted person. Brother John told me that one time, on a tour in South America, Alvin had to do the live singing because Brother John couldn't make the tour and Lou Gossett, who replaced him, couldn't sing because he would get distracted watching the dancers. Once Alvin was dancing *Back-water Blues* with Hope Clarke. I remember asking, "Who's that singing?" It was Alvin. He must have gone down to the pit and then back up to dance. His singing was better than adequate. If he had studied, he probably could have developed a great voice.

He made you feel that you were an important part of the company. I was probably the only dancer who ever had maternity leave with this company. He made me know that I had a place to come back to. When my son was born in February 1972, Alvin called the following week and asked if I needed anything. He said, "I'm doing the programming for City Center. When do you think you'll be able to dance?" I said, "Alvin, I haven't been able to find my arabesque. I don't know if I can do more than sit on a stool. I may have to sit this season out. Will it be okay if I come back in June when things start up again for the summer?" He said, "You know you're a very important part of this company, but I guess we'll have to do this one without you." Now, for a small company, one of the worst things that can happen is turnover and losing dancers. I was allowed not only to have a child and be guaranteed a job but to have an additional couple of months. It was incredible, phenomenal. It was because Alvin was warm and giving.

Carmen de Lavallade

I can't remember when Alvin and I really became friends. In school Alvin was a mysterious kind of young man and very quiet. We just sort of migrated toward one another. He was on the gymnastics team. I saw this gorgeous guy doing these free exercises. At that time I was studying dance, and he really looked like a dancer. He was doing something different than what the other fellows were doing. I told him, "You ought to be a dancer." I had no idea what would follow after I put that germ of an idea in his head. One time he hold me that it was all my fault that he was in dance.

Even then Alvin had a way of appearing and disappearing. He was there one day and we looked up and he was gone. We'd say, "Where's Alvin?" He had gone off someplace and would eventually come back. That's what I mean by mysterious. Our friendship really started at the Lester Horton School. And it was when Lester passed that Alvin and I really became close. All of us kind of bonded together as a family. I'm so glad that we had a family get-together about three years ago and Alvin came. We were surprised that he had made the effort.

Alvin was unique as a performer. I don't think he looked like anybody else on the stage, but more like a stevedore. At the same time he had a vulnerability, which is a very good combination. The last time we danced together was on a tour to Southeast Asia in 1962. We were doing a duet from *Blues Suite*. Before the tour I was taking acting classes with Stella Adler. I think Alvin was, too. We were in our acting phase at that time. I remember the first rehearsal when we got the first part of the dance piece. It really wasn't dancing at all. It was acting. We had a wonderful time. It was his gem, his best piece, that duet. When we performed it at the Boston Common, we thought, "Oh, dear, people are not going to like this." We liked it but didn't know how they would respond. It was real old blues sung by Brother John Sellers. We also had a bass and guitar. Well, we tore Boston Commons up, absolutely tore it up.

Then came one of those things that happens in life that you can't control. We went on tour to Southeast Asia as the de Lavallade-Ailey American Dance Company. At the time I was kind of known more than Alvin. I think he was a bit upset about the name because as we landed in different places we were the Alvin Ailey Company, then we turned around and it was the de Lavallade-Ailey Company. Finally I said to Alvin, "Make up your mind about what you're going to call us. It doesn't make any difference to me what it is. Let's just get it straightened out." By the time we got back, it was the Ailey Company starring Carmen de Lavallade. I really didn't care one way or another, but it was kind of embarrassing to me because people would ask, "Carmen, what is it? Is it this or is it that?" I knew Alvin wanted his own company. He was like a brother to me, but he was a bit of a mystery. He couldn't deal with problems. He would just throw his hands up and run, but I was used to that. I must say I was pleased that we always stayed friends through thick and thin. I'm not the kind of person to hold grudges. We went through too much together as a kind of family. Those kinds of things you can't forget or let go.

I think Alvin's best work was that little blues duet we did together. That was his crown. I think he was considering reviving it. I told him that he should. We were wonderful together, a real match. Alvin, because of something in his background, wasn't afraid to use popular music to make a concert statement. And his movements were not nightclubby. They had a vitality. At that time, you didn't see people move onstage the way his dancers did. Now you see it all the time.

I loved him. He was a wonderful, wonderful person who left too soon. I'm sorry we didn't see each other more often. That's why my last moment with Alvin was so precious. That was the last time I got to talk to him. We talked about old times, about high school, about standing on corners waiting for buses, about all those funny, silly things that you think of when talking about your past.

Lula Elizabeth Cooper, Alvin's mother

Alvin was born at home on the fifth of January. It was cold as the dickens. We had a potbelly stove. When I went into labor, my sister went and got Dr. Flanagan. He was white. There weren't any black doctors in our area. He examined me and said, "She's not ready yet, but I'm not going back to my office. I'll just stay all night." There was a couch near the bed where he could lay down. The only thing he told them to do was to get him a cup to spit in because he dipped snuff. About five o'clock in the morning the pains started hitting me. They started boiling water and getting towels. About five-thirty in the morning on the fifth of January there was Alvin Ailey. I never went to the doctor while I was pregnant, and Alvin never moved the whole time. When the doctor came to deliver him, I said, "Either I'm carrying around a dead young'un or this is the laziest young'un a pregnant woman ever had to carry." I think he weighed six to eight pounds at birth and was twenty-one inches long. He was a big baby, and he got busy as soon as he was born. The next day, his eyes opened. Dr. Flanagan was still there. He said, "Can you imagine? That boy's looking' all around." I said, "Ain't all babies supposed to do that?" He said, "No way. They sleep." That boy had his eyes open.

We moved a lot when Alvin was young because I was looking for work. We lived in Rogers, then left there and went to Milano. From Milano we went to Wharton. When we left Wharton, we went to Navasota, and from there we went to Los Angeles. I was doing mostly housework wherever I could get it. I worked for a while in a hospital in Navasota.

I remember once we were on a bus that stopped in a little place called Hearn, Texas. Alvin was about three or four. When we got off the bus for a snack, the place set aside for black people to eat was one table next to a row of toilets. He was glad to eat, but he didn't care too much about being so close to the toilets. I didn't think about it much then, but you look back and people coming in off six buses and using the toilet right next to where you are eating a hamburger. Isn't that awful?

When we lived in Wharton, Alvin would go out every morning and pick wildflowers and give them to me. I think he was beginning to realize how hard I was working. I was picking cotton. I would fix food, and Alvin, who was about five then, would sit down to eat and leave a lot of food on his plate. If I turned my back, Alvin was gone and so was the plate. This went on for three or four days. Finally, one morning after breakfast I decided to see what he was doing with the food. I saw him going under the house. When I peeped under the house, that little boy was feeding the biggest chicken snake you ever saw in your life. That scared me to death. The snake was eating out of his hand. He was giving that snake his biscuit, his bacon, whatever he had. I told him he'd better stop giving food bought by my hard-earned money to snakes.

Another time, there was a beautiful little tree by our porch.

It was just so green and pretty. So this little fellow of mine went
out there one day and shook the tree. All these green things
came off. He said, "Come here, Mommy, all the leaves fell off
the tree." I looked, and saw not leaves, but praying mantises,
millions of them. He was picking them up. I said, "Boy, put
them things down." I was so afraid of them. Alvin was very
adventurous.

He was always looking for something odd. One day he
found this little stick that was made like a chicken breast. He
said, "Look Mommy, ain't this cute?" I asked him what it was.
He said, "It's a cottee." I didn't know what that was, and he
didn't know, but that's what he called it. I kept the darned thing.
I might still have it somewhere. In Rogers, Texas, you couldn't
go to school until you were six, but Alvin's cousins would take
him along with them when he was still five. He was so darn
smart. The teacher was amazed that he could recite his ABCs
forward and then sing them backward. Multiplication tables, he
could sing those, too. I guess he learned from his cousins.

He was baptized by Reverand Sandy Taplin when he was
seven in what we called a tank, a mudhole. They call them lakes
now. It was man-built for people to get baptized in. The pastor
would take the child out into this muddy hole while the deacons
had sticks to run the water moccasins away so he could get the
baptism done. The people on the bank were singing "Wade in
the water, children. God's gonna trouble the water." That's
where that came from in *Revelations*. After the baptisms, they'd
put their dry clothes back on, and we'd all go back into the
church and pray. Then we would lead a song we wanted to sing.
After Alvin's baptism, I remember this lady named Hattie Taplin
broke out singing "I Been 'Buked, I Been Scorned." That's
where he got that from in *Revelations*.

The train blowing the whistle in *Blues Suite* Alvin got when
we lived in Rogers. That was the only place where he would be

able to hear them because we didn't live too far from the railroad tracks. I don't know anywhere else he was close to a railroad track.

Besides going to school in Rogers, he also belonged to the Baptist Student Union at church. If a Sunday school teacher said something wrong, Alvin would raise his hand and correct her if he knew she was wrong. Once he asked, "Is Jesus one fellow— God one and Christ another?" I'd say, "Shut up, boy." But you knew that was a heck of a question for a child to ask.

During this time he was as fat as an ox. I don't know which side of the family he got that from. There are some big people in my family. My daddy was six feet tall, but he was very lean. I don't remember my mother, but they told me she was kind of plump. My half sister was also kind of plump. I've always been lean.

After we moved to Navasota, Texas, I met Amos Alexander. He became my boyfriend. He was about thirty years older than me, but he was nice to us. He considered Alvin his son and acted like a father to him. Amos had lots of music in his house. He had all kinds of records that Alvin loved to play on Amos's old-time Victrola with the white dog on top looking in the horn. He also had a piano Alvin used to pluck on. While living with Amos, I got a job at Memorial Hospital. Alvin went to school and played that big old horn in the band. When I left Navasota to go to California in January, Alvin stayed with Amos until June, when school was out. He was twelve years old when we moved to Los Angeles.

He was already in junior high school, and I enrolled him in George Washington Carver Junior High School. His history teacher there was a cousin of mine named Lois Rabb. Alvin always liked to teach, starting in his Sunday school days, so sometimes when Lois went to lunch or had to be out of the classroom, she turned the history class over to him. He went on to Thomas Jefferson High School, where he was practically always an A student. From there he went to UCLA and then to San Francisco State. He got a job interpreting Spanish for the Greyhound Bus Company.

Alvin was always good at languages. He learned Spanish from Spanish kids back in Texas. In Los Angeles I remember a Chinese fellow who had a little grocery store. He had two or three girls and a son, whom Alvin made it his business to make friends with. Soon he was speaking some Chinese that he learned from them. Eventually he went on to speak six languages.

Alvin used to do a lot of writing and tear it up and put it in the wastebasket. I told him, "If you are going to keep on doing that, you're going to have to empty these wastebaskets yourself." He was a bit messy, but he was constantly doing something with a pencil. I remember one time he told me that I didn't have to clean up his room that day. "I'll do it." Like any mother I wondered what in the world was in his room. When he went off to school, I kept thinking about it. Finally, I eased into his room and saw a great big bowl of water with a damn snake in it. It scared the hell out of me. When I asked him about it, he said it was for a science class.

It must have had been two years Alvin had been taking dance lessons with Lester Horton before I learned about it. He said he was helping his teachers at UCLA, but all the time he was going to Lester Horton. I hated the idea. I refused to go see what he was doing for the longest time—I didn't know he was doing decent work. Finally, I decided to go see *Mourning Morning,* and after seeing that I got interested. I told him to "go after it. Do the best you can. Be sure you do good work. And whatever you do, don't get too big for your britches. Remember where you came from. Don't forget to pray. The prayer I mean is very short, and it's in the Bible, "Our father which art in heaven.""

Then turn over to Psalms 150 and say, "Make a joyful noise unto the Lord with your harps, your piano, your guitar, everything." It says that right in the Bible. Alvin has been going after it ever since.

When they called him to come to New York City and do *House of Flowers,* I like to have died. I didn't want him to go. It was too far away from home. I thought he'd be hungry. Every week I'd send him half of my little salary. He'd say, "Momma, I'm eating. Don't send me no money." I sent it anyway. One good thing is that he calls from wherever he is, the Islands, Paris—wherever he goes he calls me.

The only thing that worries me is, he needs to take time for himself. He should stop ripping and running and realize that he is just one human being and his body and soul can only take so much. Learn how to say no. Everybody's having a ball, and he's flat on his back. Overworked. Who knows what will happen if he continues on the pace he's on, he can't do it, just no way. It's impossible. Even with the type of work he does, there is a time for rest. When a person works as hard as Alvin has worked and goes to bed, he's still wide awake, and then has to take a pill to go to sleep. That's no way to live. Why does he have to fill his body with chemicals in order to sleep? He should keep his body and mind in such a condition that after a day's work, he'll be able to take a shower, have dinner or whatever, and go right on to sleep. The need for chemicals is a sign that he's tired, under too much pressure with too much to think about. He's going to have to do much better as far as his health is concerned. He's going to have to start thinking about himself.

Acknowledgments

$\mathcal{A}$fter Alvin Ailey's death a bunch of people provided the financial, spiritual, and technical support that enabled me to carry out Alvin's goal. I thank Bob Gumbs for steering me to Gary Fitzgerald at Carol Publishing Group, who had the editorial vision to see that Alvin Ailey deserved an opportunity to present his life and his creative genius in his own words. Thanks and acknowledgment also go to Jim Ellison, whose editing was crucial to the project, and to Alvin's mother, Mrs. Lula Cooper, who knew of her son's desire to tell his story and who cooperated in seeing that it was realized.

Thanks and acknowledgment also to my father, Upson Bailey Sr., Gloria and John Spencer, Zana and Elijudah Jones, and Marian and Bruce Scott, my sisters and brothers-in-law, and my niece, Sherry Tillman. Also to friends and colleagues, such as Earl Grant, Bess Daniels, Monroe Fredericks, Dennis Harvey, Leslie Branch, Lloyd Williams, S. Karie Nabinet, Claudia Jermott, Hazel Trice Edney, Ishmail Conway, Marie Brown, Paulette J. Haskins, T. C. Milner, Mark Edwards, Kathleen Rose, Mickey Board, Sandy Callahan, Reggie Johnson, Mrs. Alice Jackson Stuart, Tracy Sherrod, Frank Solomon, Bill Mackey, Al Reid, and pastors Roscoe Cooper, Barbara Ingram, and Kenneth Watkins and other members of the Metropolitan African American Baptist Church.

Special thanks go to Bernice Bryant and Angela Smith, who came through at crunch time when I needed the manuscript put on the computer. Finally I thank my grandchildren Tiarra, Juliya, and Dominique, who are the future.

Index

Lester Horton: Modern Dance Pioneer
  (Warren), 51
Lester Horton Dance Theater, 45,
  60
Lester Horton group, 103
Lewitzky, Bella, 50, 52, 58, 59, 60
Liberian Suite (Ellington), 55
Limón, Jose, 78
Lincoln Center for the Performing
  Arts, 7, 113
Lincoln Theater, 34, 113, 130
lithium, 144, 146
Logan, Joshua, 84–87
London Festival Ballet, 7
Lorca, Garcia, 117
Los Angeles theater district, 39–42
Los Angeles years, 31–42, 169–70
Lucky, 139, 143
Lydia Bailey, 80

McBeth, Robert, 85
McCarthy hearings, 59
McCullers, Carson, 118–19
McKayle, Donnie, 78, 80, 122
McNeil, Claudia, 85–87, 112
McShann, Jay, 129
Magdelena, 40
Manchester, P. W., 96
manic phase, 137, 141
manic-depression, 134, 138,
  143–44
marijuana, 136–43, 147–48
Marinoff, Fania, 118
Marshall, Minnie, 83, 88, 94, 103,
  108, 156
Martin, Don, 61, 69, 103
Martin, John, 92
Maslow, Sophie, 80
Mason, Audrey, 81, 90, 96
Mass (Bernstein), 7

Maxon, Normand, 94, 95, 96
Mean Ol' Frisco, 84
Memoria (Ailey), 136, 137
Merrick, David, 82
Messel, Oliver, 73
method actor, 83, 88
Metropolitan Opera, 7
Metropolitan Opera House, 113
Michael's Studio, 90
Minskoff Building, 136
Miss Julie, 116
Mitchell, Arthur, 74, 76, 77, 79,
  117, 120, 127
Montalban, Ricardo, 81
Montoya, Mary, 74
mood swings, 137
Moore, Charles, 90, 92, 94, 96,
  104, 156
Mourning Morning, 65, 66, 170
"Move, Members, Move," 99
Mozart, Wolfgang Amadeus, 43
My People, 107, 108, 109, 114

Nash, Joe, 6, 157–58
National Endowment for the Arts,
  130, 134, 150
Neal, Charles, 94
New York City Ballet, 76, 120,
  121
New York City Center, 102
New York modern dance scene, 77
New York State Council on the
  Arts, 134
Nicks, Walter, 79
Ninety Degrees in the Shade, 128
Nixon, Richard M., 114
Nuyorican Poets Cafe, 138–39, 152

Oka, Michihiko, 128
Orozco, 64, 100